THE ULTIMATE GUIDE TO
WHITEWATER
RAFTING
AND RIVER CAMPING

MOLLY ABSOLON

Guilford, Connecticut

FALCON®

An imprint of The Rowman & Littlefield Publishing Group, Inc.
4501 Forbes Blvd., Ste. 200
Lanham, MD 20706
www.rowman.com

Falcon and FalconGuides are registered trademarks and Make Adventure Your Story is a trademark of Rowman & Littlefield.

Distributed by NATIONAL BOOK NETWORK

Copyright © 2018 The Rowman & Littlefield Publishing Group, Inc.

Photos by Matt Leidecker unless noted otherwise

British Library Cataloguing in Publication Information available

Library of Congress Cataloging-in-Publication Data available

ISBN 978-1-4930-3233-4 (paperback)
ISBN 978-1-4930-3234-1 (e-book)

∞™ The paper used in this publication meets the minimum requirements of American National Standard for Information Sciences—Permanence of Paper for Printed Library Materials, ANSI/NISO Z39.48-1992.

Printed in the United States of America

The author and Rowman & Littlefield assume no liability for accidents happening to, or injuries sustained by, readers who engage in the activities described in this book.

CONTENTS

ACKNOWLEDGMENTS

ALTHOUGH I HAVE BEEN LUCKY ENOUGH to raft a lot of rivers, and have gained a lot of knowledge doing so, I still don't consider myself an expert rafter. To make this book a reality I relied on the advice and guidance of people I admire and respect for their whitewater boating skills, wilderness river trip experience, and rafting expertise. These people include Allison Berg, Margaret Creel, Brian Goldberg, Ari Kotler, Julie Mueller, Don Sharaf, and Kat Smithhammer. They each brought years of river experience to the book through their input. As a group, they include private rafters, professional rafters, raft instructors, and even the owner of a commercial rafting company—SOAR Northwest. All of them took hours of their personal time to wade through my manuscript checking for accuracy, offering suggestions, and generally just making sure I was on the right track. I am very grateful for their generous help.

I also want to thank Matt Liedecker for his amazing photos. As always, photos make a book like this and I appreciate his skill and the beauty of his images. In addition to Matt, Ari Kotler, Dot Newton, Eric Riley, Eric Scranton, Stefanie Vandaele, Moe Witschard, and Tom Zell provided a few extra photographs to fill in the holes, and my daughter, Avery Absolon, drew the diagrams. Thanks!

Finally, I want to recognize the people I've been down rivers with who aren't included in the list above. There are too many to list, but a few regulars deserve mention: Tim, Erin, and Charlie Burnham; Rachael Price; Mark, Gavin, and Jasper Roy; Georgie Stanley; Ben Hammond; Lisa Johnson; Michael Wehrle; Michelle Williamson. Plus, of course, there's my husband, Allen O'Bannon, who opened up the river world to an old climber, and Avery Absolon, who is rapidly becoming a boater in her own right.

INTRODUCTION

MY DAUGHTER WAS THREE WHEN WE FIRST FLOATED the Main Salmon River in central Idaho. I wasn't much of a boater, so my primary job was to hold on to her and to the raft when we went through the rapids.

The weather was terrible. It was August and my friends told me to expect temperatures in the 80s or 90s during the day, so I packed lightly. But it was raining when we got to the put-in, and for the next three days temperatures never got much above 50 degrees. We wore all our clothes and stopped at lunch to rig up a shelter, start a stove, and make hot chocolate for the kids. I'll never forget watching them—we had six kids under eight years old on that adventure—playing in the rain, their slickers covered in wet sand. They didn't care. They built castles and fished. They ran up and down the beach, creating their own games. We read them stories and kept them well fed. They looked like drowned rats, but they were laughing and smiling and having a blast well before the sun finally came out and warmed us up.

That trip hooked me. I'd been having a hard time figuring out how to backpack with my daughter without carrying a monster pack or hiring horses or llamas to heft the load. River trips meant our gear was on the raft, not on my back. It meant the kids didn't have to cover long miles on their feet. We weren't constantly cajoling them with candy to keep them walking. Instead we sat in the raft, laughing and screaming our way through the whitewater and lounging back watching the scenery slip past when it was calm.

Once the temperatures heated up, we swam and had water fights. We sunbathed on the back of the raft and took turns rowing. It was six days of bliss. The stresses of home were far away. We had no cell coverage or electronics, so no social media distractions. We got up in the morning, ate a huge meal, drank our coffee, loaded up, and drifted downstream. At the end of the day, we set up camp on a beach, made cocktails, ate a huge dinner, and went to bed. I left the river wishing I could stay out there forever.

A friend of mine who routinely floats the Colorado River through the Grand Canyon calls what I described above "river time." It's that sense of living totally

River trips are a great way to bring family and friends together away from the stress and distractions of daily life.

in the moment, surrounded by beautiful nature with no cares in the world. It's hard to get that feeling in modern life—there are just too many distractions, obligations, and things on your to-do list. But on rivers you can find it.

River trips run the gamut from Class I casual floats to Class V whitewater. Obviously the difficulty of the river affects the nature of your trip and the level

Your river trip can be a simple flat-water float or a raging whitewater run, depending on your skill and desires.

Multiday river trips take you deep into the earth's wildest river corridors.
STEFANIE VANDAELE

of skill and expertise you need to run it. On some rivers you will have a fabulous time with kids; on others the difficulty and danger may make it smarter to leave them at home. Regardless of the challenge, all river trips are unified by that feeling of river time. Everyone comes back reinvigorated and ready for more.

This book is written for newer rafters looking to put together their own multiday river trip. It's not a substitute for experience, rather a supplement to help you solidify your skills. We'll talk a little bit about rafting technique and equipment, and provide an introduction to reading water and running rapids, but those skills are best learned from a more experienced mentor.

For that reason, it's a good idea to make your first excursions with people who have been there and done that. Ask lots of questions. Follow them through rapids. Get someone to sit in your raft and coach you through a run. Take a class or go with a guide.

This book comes in handy after you get home from these experiences and you want to solidify the concepts that were thrown at you in the middle of a rapid's chaos. There, in the comfort of your living room, you can refer to this book to analyze what you saw on the river and think about what was actually

It can take years to gain the skills you need to safely run Class V whitewater like Devil Creek Rapid on the South Fork of the Salmon River in Idaho.

happening to you in your raft. Together with a good teacher and time spent in a raft, this book will help you become an independent boater who doesn't need to rely on more experienced friends to take a multiday raft trip.

This book also covers the ins and outs of river camping. There are all sorts of ways to approach living on a river. You can pile on the gear and bring along a special outfit for every day of the trip, as well as games, musical instruments, cocktails, fresh veggies, and meat and potatoes. You name it: With a big enough raft, you can probably bring it, plus the kitchen sink.

Or you can borrow principles from lightweight backpackers and reduce your load so you need fewer rafts for your team and can be more efficient and nimble both on the water and getting in and out of camp. We'll talk about both approaches—there are pluses and minuses to either option—and include gear lists, packing tips, cooking suggestions, and expedition planning guidelines.

This book touches on basic river rescue and safety. But if you plan to do challenging river trips, we highly recommend you take a swiftwater rescue course. Again, think of this book as your cheat sheet—a reference or reminder for when you get home and want to contemplate the rescue skills you've acquired in a class.

Finally, we have included a list of some of the most coveted river trips in the world. Probably every rafter you talk to will have at least one or two of these

Becoming a proficient rafter allows you to undertake multiday river trips with people of all ages and experience levels.

trips on his or her bucket list. The rivers we've chosen are included because of their scenic beauty, the quality of the whitewater, the camping, and their conduciveness to creating the sense of river time we all seek when we turn off our phones and slip our rafts into the current.

The best river trips in the world are known not only for their rapids, but also for their beautiful settings and incredible wilderness camping.

WHITEWATER RAFTING BASICS

RAFTING HISTORY

Humans have used rafts to navigate waterways for thousands of years. Early rafts were made by lashing together logs, reeds, planks, and other pieces of wood to make a floating platform for transporting people and cargo over water. For the most part these rafts were used on flat water, but in 1811 the Overland Astorians, a group of fur trappers traversing the American West, tried to use a raft to descend the Snake River in Wyoming. The river's rapids proved too dangerous and difficult for the craft, and the Snake became known as the "Mad River," a moniker that is used today by one of the Snake's commercial outfitters.

In 1842, Lieutenant John Frémont and his assistant, Horace H. Day, created a raft made of rubber to explore the Platte River. The flexibility of the raft made it easier to manage in turbulent water, and Frémont's boat is considered to be the prototype of a modern rubber raft.

But the Platte River expedition did not result in a revolution in whitewater boating. The first real whitewater river trip was John Wesley Powell's famous Journey of Discovery down the Green and Colorado Rivers in 1869. Powell's party used wooden boats for their expedition, so it wasn't a raft trip, and they lined most of the rapids, but it did begin to open the door to the idea of using boats to explore wild rivers.

In Idaho, boatmen used wooden scows to descend the Salmon River from the onset of European settlement. Early trips stopped in Shoup, upriver of today's Main Salmon run; there the boats were dismantled to be sold as lumber and boaters returned upstream by road. But in 1896, Harry Guleke took his scow 152 miles downstream to Riggins, proving the entire river could be navigated.

One of the earliest known recreational whitewater trips occurred in Utah in 1934, when Norm Neville and his new bride went on a honeymoon trip down the San Juan River. Four years later he guided paying clients down the Grand Canyon in what he called a "cataract boat," which he designed and built specifically for the expedition. In 1939, Amos Berg ran a rubber raft down the Salmon River, and the following year the first commercially guided group made the trip. After that the industry slowly grew, with more and more companies offering whitewater adventures on rivers.

The influx of military surplus rubber rafts, however, really changed the world of whitewater boating. Rubber rafts had been used as landing craft and to create pontoon bridges in World War II and the Korean war. After these conflicts ended, surplus rafts and pontoons flooded the market. Don Hatch and his father Bus were among the first to recognize the value of rubber rafts for commercial river running. They saw that the inflatable boats could carry lots of passengers, that they bounced off rocks, and that they were easy to store—plus, after the wars, they were abundant and cheap. Within a few years inflatable boats had become wildly popular among river runners and the era of commercial raft trips began.

Millions of people enjoy whitewater rafting for its excitement, challenge, and the beautiful places it takes them.

Rafts come in a variety of sizes and shapes. What works best for you will depend on your goals and budget.

Ultimately it was the inclusion of whitewater boating in the 1972 Munich Olympics that marked a turning point for the sport and cemented its place in the general public's imagination. After those Olympics commercial whitewater rafting took off.

In 2014, 3.8 million people went whitewater rafting, according to the "Special Report on Paddlesports 2015." Rafting is the third-most popular paddle sport, behind kayaking and canoeing. In fourth place, stand-up paddleboarding is quickly gaining popularity. Rafting participation rates have stagnated somewhat in recent years as people discover other ways to navigate rivers and run whitewater, but rafting remains the primary way people enjoy multiday river trips.

Modern rafts come in a variety of sizes, materials, and even shapes. Most of them tend to have the classic oval shape we associate with the idea of a raft, but catarafts, which are made from two tubes held together by a frame, are also common. Rafts are popular for a number of reasons: They are stable, fun, and relatively forgiving. Plus they can take you, your friends, and your gear to places that aren't easily accessible without a boat.

Rafts are one of the safest crafts for navigating whitewater and are, therefore, a great way for beginners to get into the sport of whitewater boating. Still, boat-

RENT OR BUY?

One of the first questions to ask yourself as your interest in whitewater rafting develops is whether you want to rent or buy a raft. Many river companies rent fully outfitted rafts for day or multiday use. The advantage of this is that you can rent all the necessary gear—frames, oars, paddles, life jackets, etc.—and have it waiting for you at the put-in and whisked away from you at the takeout. You probably won't even have to clean out your portable toilet at the end of your trip if you go this route. The disadvantage is that renting a raft with all the necessary accoutrements is expensive. The rate for a 15-foot raft rental for a six-day Main Salmon River trip in 2017 was roughly $2,000, plus $250 for a kitchen package. For a three-week Grand Canyon trip, rental rates for a raft and kitchen start at around $5,000.

Most high-quality whitewater rafts retail for several thousand dollars depending on the size you opt for, plus there are countless essentials—oars, frame, paddles, etc.—that add to the cost. By the time you get fully decked out, you are probably looking at dropping anywhere from $10,000 to as much as $15,000 on your setup. If you plan to take a lot of river trips each year, that investment is worthwhile. If you think you are only going to go on one trip a summer, renting becomes more appealing, especially when you consider the cost of maintenance together with the time and effort required to prep for and clean up after your trip. Storing and transporting gear is also an issue when you own it.

That said, owning a raft gives you greater freedom over the location and timing of your next trip. If that is your goal, you may be in the market. Plus, having your own raft can get you invited on more river trips!

ing Class III whitewater or harder is challenging, and takes skill and practice, so it should always be pursued with humility and guidance.

NARROWING YOUR OPTIONS

There's no one-size-fits-all raft that serves every function perfectly, so it's helpful to identify your goals and objectives to ensure you end up with a boat that serves most of your needs well. Make sure you establish your budget before you get down to shopping. It's easy to get talked into something that is bigger, flashier, and more expensive than you really need or can afford if you don't do your homework before you set out to make your purchase.

For some river trips, such as a long Grand Canyon trip, many people opt to rent all their rafts and equipment to simplify logistics.
MOLLY ABSOLON

To help you narrow down your options, ask yourself the following questions:

1. What do you want to do with your raft (whitewater, day trips, multiday outings, family adventures, fishing)?
2. How often do you plan to use it?
3. Where do you intend to use your raft (what part of the country; what types of rivers)?
4. How many people do you want to carry or support (i.e., do you need to carry gear for kayakers or other members of your group in addition to those individuals who will be riding on the boat)?
5. How long are the trips you plan to use the raft on?
6. What experience do you have, and in what kind of rafts? What types of rafts do you see on the waterways you intend to travel?
7. Do you plan to paddle, row, or paddle and row the raft?
8. Is raft weight a consideration (for flights, portaging, storage, etc.)?
9. How much can you spend?

Once you've answered these questions you will be a more informed and savvy consumer, and you'll be able to help a salesperson guide you to the right raft for your needs.

ANATOMY OF A RAFT

Rafts are generally made with four air-filled chambers separated by baffles inside the raft's exterior tubes.

Most modern rafts are made with four air-filled chambers and an inflatable, self-bailing floor.

Paddle rafts will also have air-filled thwarts that run between the outside tubes to help with rigidity and provide a place for passengers to sit or paddlers to brace. Most rafts these days come with an inflatable, self-bailing floor that allows water to run out freely rather than having to bail after every rapid. Non-self-bailers—or bucket boats—are disappearing rapidly, so we won't go into any details about them here. But they do have one advantage: They are much lighter than rafts with a self-bailing floor. If you are flying into a river with your raft—such as in the Arctic—bucket boats may be a better choice because of the weight factor.

Paddle rafts include inflatable thwarts between the tubes. These thwarts help provide structure to the raft and give paddlers a place to sit and brace.

Usually rafts are rigged with an outside line—called a grab or perimeter line—that runs between D rings on the tubes. The line gives you something to grab onto if you come out of the boat or if you need to carry it up onto a beach or around a rapid. Make sure the grab line is secured snugly so no slack can entangle a foot or body part in the event of a capsize.

You'll also want a line on the bow of your raft to tie it up when you are onshore, so the raft can't drift away if the wind or water comes up. Give yourself 50 feet or so of rope so you have plenty of length to secure the raft to trees, rocks, or a sand stake well back from the waterline. Some people prefer to carry two shorter ropes—one stored away, the other attached to a D ring on the bow—so they don't have to contend with a long, potentially tangled mess of rope when all they need is 20 feet to secure the raft to a log. You may find that the length of your bowline will be determined by the nature of the river you are on. For small rivers in heavily wooded areas, you won't need as long a line as you will need on big desert rivers, where the beaches are sandy and wide.

Bowlines can be stuffed into a bag for storage or they can be coiled and tucked under the grab line. The key is to make sure the line is readily accessible, without a lot of loose rope that could become an entrapment hazard in the water.

A line on the front (and sometimes the back) of your boat allows you to secure your raft when you are onshore.

If you plan to paddle your raft, there's not much else to be done for its setup. Some rafts have foot cups to help paddlers maintain a secure position in the boat in big whitewater, but for most rivers, paddlers can get a good-enough position by wedging their feet under the thwarts and side tubes.

To complete your setup for an oar rig, you need a frame for the oars and some kind of seat for the rower. We'll go into more details about that later.

Size

Rafts range in size from personal inflatable kayaks to ones that are 30 feet or longer. The rafts at either end of this size spectrum tend to be specialty crafts designed for specific purposes such as carrying large loads, using motors or for solo boating. For the purposes of this book, we will focus on rafts between 12 to 18 feet long that are typically used for multiday whitewater rafting trips.

For shallow, fast rivers, rafts in the 12- to 14-foot range are nice because of their maneuverability. A party of three people or fewer can make a 12- to 14-foot raft work on a three- to four-day trip, but if you have more people or plan a longer trip, you may need something bigger. Larger rafts—say 16- to 18-footers—provide more cargo space and more room for people to lounge around on the tubes on slower parts of the river.

You see all kinds of inflatable crafts on rivers. Each is designed for a specific purpose, including this makeshift raft to help backpackers navigate flat water.

Today's rafts come with either traditional I-beam floor construction or drop-stitch floors like this one. It's worth trying both to see which you prefer if you are in the market for a raft.

Small rafts are more maneuverable than big ones, and the ride is often more exciting than the ride in a big raft that can plow through waves and holes without getting bounced around as much. That also means small rafts tend to be a bit tippier and easier to flip in rapids.

Width, tube diameter, and rocker are also considerations. In general, wider rafts with larger tubes are going to be less likely to flip than rafts that are the same length but narrower, or the same length but with smaller tubes. The more rocker you have in your raft, the easier it is to spin, which is advantageous in technical whitewater, but does make tracking—or keeping your boat straight—more challenging in flat water.

Finally, boats now come with a choice between I-beam floors—floors with baffles that create ridges—and drop-stitch floors. Drop-stitch floors use the same technology used in inflatable stand-up paddleboards, which creates a flat, more rigid floor than I-beam construction. People have varying opinions on the pros and cons of the different floor types. In general, most people say rafts with I-beam floors tend to track better, while the drop-stitch floor provides a more rigid platform, which is nice if you like to stand to row and don't have floor-boards. Drop-stitch floors are laced into the bottom of the raft, which makes them easier to cut out in an emergency or lash gear to for security.

Paddle rafts versus oar rigs

Paddle rafting enables lots of people to participate in propelling the raft downstream and through rapids. It's fun, challenging, and allows people to be more involved than they would be if they were just lounging about while their buddy rows.

On moderate rivers, paddlers can be relatively inexperienced as long as you have a skilled paddle captain and fit participants who can follow orders and paddle hard. On more difficult rivers and technical whitewater, all paddlers should be skilled and able to work together efficiently as a team to successfully navigate challenging rapids that require precise moves.

Another option, if you want people to paddle, is to combine rowing and paddling by putting a stern-mount oar frame on the back of your raft. The oars give the raft guide more control and enable less-experienced crews to tackle harder rapids than they could with just paddle power.

Paddle rafts allow more people to actively participate in the act of moving the raft downstream, but they don't carry as much gear as oar rigs.

BASIC GUIDELINES FOR BUYING THE RIGHT RAFT

1. If your goal is to only paddle your raft on day trips, figure that a 12- to 13-foot raft will be comfortable for a maximum of six paddlers. A 14- to 15-foot raft works well for up to eight. More people? Go bigger.
2. For a weeklong trip with two people and an oar rig setup, you'll want at least a 13-foot raft. For three or four people on the same trip, you need to up the size to 14 or 15 feet. For high volume rivers, a 15- to 18-foot raft will be more stable. Bigger rafts also mean more room for cargo and people.

The downside to paddle rafts on multiday trips is that it's hard to carry a lot of gear, along with your paddle crew, in one raft. You can do it, but you need to think like a backpacker and go light unless you have a gear raft along for support.

Oar rigs are perfect for carrying a load. Depending on the size of the raft, they can carry hundreds of pounds of equipment as well as a couple of passengers. Oar rigs require at least one competent rower to negotiate rapids. On flat water almost everyone can take a hand at the oars to help row the boat downstream.

Oar rigs can carry lots of gear and passengers, making them the perfect workhorse for a multiday river trip.

Catarafts versus rafts

Historically, most people start rafting in classic oval-shaped rafts, but catarafts are gaining popularity and are more and more common on rivers these days. Both styles of rafts have their enthusiastic fans, and both work really well for certain functions and less well for others. The choice between the two often depends on personal preference and the style of trip you tend to take.

In general, properly loaded catarafts are faster and more maneuverable than oval-shaped rafts and for these reasons they make a great play boat and are nice in highly technical water—

but the caveat "properly loaded" is important. It's easy to put too much weight on a cataraft, and an overloaded cat is sluggish and hard to handle. Furthermore, the weight distribution in a cat is critical to its performance, so packing one takes a bit more care than packing a raft.

Catarafts are faster and more maneuverable than traditional rafts, making them the rafting version of a play boat.

Some catarafts are designed to be paddled, but these rafts generally can't carry a lot of gear.

A cat's open design means you don't have to worry about taking on water in rapids. But no floor also means it's easy to lose stuff if you aren't careful. Cats are less passenger-friendly than rafts because there are fewer places for people to sit and it's hard to move around on a cat while on the water.

Rafts with floors are easier to load than catarafts. You don't need to worry as much about weight distribution affecting performance, and it's easy to pile things up in the bow and stern of the boat. Rafts can be either rowed or paddled, and they have a lot of room for passengers, which makes them more kid-friendly. Some catarafts are designed to be paddled—usually by two or four people—but for the most part a paddled cat cannot carry much in the way of gear. It's more for playing than transporting cargo.

Rafts have more surface contact with the water because of their floors, which can make them less maneuverable than a cat and can cause rafts to hang up more readily on submerged rocks. However, if a cat and a raft are carrying the same amount of weight, cat tubes will sit lower in the water than the raft, meaning cat has more draft and can get stuck in shallow water sooner than a raft.

Finally, rafts are heavier and bulkier to transport and store than catarafts.

Traditional rafts are powerful, stable, and able to carry a lot of equipment, which means they are usually the best option for people getting into multiday river trips.

As all these pros and cons demonstrate, choosing between a cat and a raft really depends on what you want to do with your craft. Both are great options and both will open up a world of adventure for you.

BUYING A USED RAFT

You can often find great deals on preowned rafts, including rafts used by commercial rafting companies that turn over their fleets every few years. But you should be careful when buying used equipment, and if you are new to the rafting world it behooves you to go shopping with someone who can help you evaluate the deal with a seasoned eye.

In general, look for signs of wear and tear or repairs. If the boat has been patched, look carefully at the patches to see if they have been placed professionally. That means you don't see any loose edges or wrinkles. The fewer and smaller the patches, the better, since that shows the raft has had an easier life, fewer encounters with sharp objects, and a bit more TLC.

Check the handles and D rings on the boat for signs of wear. These are relatively easy to replace, but their condition can give you a clue as to the care the raft has received. If the raft color has faded significantly, beware. UV damage decreases the strength of both PVC and Hypalon. A boat that shows its years visually is more likely to puncture or tear.

A fully inflated raft should be smooth, with no cracks or wrinkles. Rough spots can indicate a coming crack. Make sure you look on the underside as well as the topside of the raft. Out of sight should not mean out of mind, especially with a boat that needs to float. If you can, do an overnight leak test to check for pinholes that allow air to escape. Inflate the boat fully and see what happens while you sleep. A fully inflated raft could be flat by morning if it has enough pinholes, which would be a real pain on overnight trips. If you can't do an overnight test, spray down the raft with soapy water and watch what happens. Pay close attention to the seams. If you have a leak, you'll see foamy bubbles forming at the site.

Check all valves, especially on older rafts, by spraying some soapy water or 303 Protectant inside the valve. Listen and look for leaking. Some valves are easy to replace; some you have to have a professional work on.

Once you've checked for leaks, let the air out of each chamber individually to make sure the internal baffles are working. Air should not move between the chambers. Similarly, if the raft has a self-bailing inflatable floor, make sure the I beams between the baffles are holding. These can be expensive and difficult to repair. If you have three or more blown I beams it may be easier to replace the floor than to try to fix it. That may not be a deal-breaker as floors are easy to replace, but it should bring the price of the raft down a lot since purchasing a new floor will be expensive.

Finally, look at the overall texture of the material. If you see worn spots or places where the outer coating has been rubbed off, check carefully for leaks. Worn spots are normal but if the raft has lots of them, it probably means you'll be doing some patching in the future. Also ask how the raft has been stored. Rafts that sit outside year-round may have UV damage, which weakens the material.

Materials

In general, rafts are made with urethane, Hypalon, or PVC. Your choice will depend on your budget, the type of boating you plan to do, and even where you live, as that may affect which rafts are readily available. There are great rafts made all over the world, but it's nice to have a local provider who can help you maintain your raft and deal with warranty issues should they arise.

Urethane or, strictly speaking, polyurethane, is a durable, lightweight, and puncture- and tear-resistant synthetic rubber. It slides over rocks well. Many users talk about urethane boats having a silky feel to them when they move through the water. Urethane tends to be expensive and stiff, making the rafts difficult to roll for storage and transport. That stiffness also makes urethane boats more prone to flipping than softer materials like Hypalon—or at least some people make this claim. Urethane boats are more difficult to field repair than other materials, but their parts are welded together making the rafts virtually indestructible.

Hypalon, a type of rubber, is easy to field repair and has a long life. It is more puncture- and abrasion-resistant than PVC, but less so than urethane. Rubber boats flex with waves, which can be good or bad depending on the particular scenario. That softness means Hypalon rafts are easier to roll up for transport than rafts made with other materials. Hypalon tends to be relatively expensive, but the rafts will last a long time.

Hypalon rafts are easier to roll up for transport than other materials.

PVC, or polyvinyl chloride, is the least expensive raft material. Some PVC rafts are mass-produced and so have been known to have quality-control issues. PVC is not particularly durable and can crack when rolled. However, unless you are a commercial rafter or do lots of trips every year, PVC boats are plenty durable for private use, will last a long time if they are properly cared for, and often have a great price tag for entry-level boats.

If the three materials mentioned above were all you had to contend with, it would be relatively easy to make a choice, but it's not that simple. Several manufacturers use a combination of materials to make their rafts. AIRE constructs its rafts with a PVC shell over a urethane bladder. Maravia makes the opposite: a urethane exterior over a PVC interior. These combinations help reduce costs and are designed to maximize the strengths and minimize the weaknesses of the materials in use.

It's great to have an understanding of these materials so you can evaluate the marketing material for a particular brand with some understanding of what they are talking about. But in general, if you go with a reputable company, you will be just fine regardless of whether the raft is urethane, Hypalon, or PVC.

To help you narrow down your options, ask your friends or see what rafts commercial rafting companies are using to get an idea of what is popular. You can also go online and read product reviews. Mountainbuzz.com hosts a forum where you can ask questions on just about anything that has to do with river running. You'll get no shortage of opinions if you start your research there.

To help determine the right raft for you, ask your friends, research online, rent different styles, and ask commercial raft companies which brand of rafts they use, and why.
DOT NEWTON

CHAPTER TWO
GETTING ON THE WATER

OAR RIGS

The person rowing the raft is usually in charge of his or her craft. He or she directs the packing and determines where and how things should be loaded onto the raft. The rower is responsible for ensuring everything is tied down and secure before launching. He or she is also usually the one who oversees the unloading process when you pull into camp. Every rower tends to have a slightly different approach to setting up his or her boat. When you first start out, it's great to copy someone else's system. As you gain experience, you can modify it to suit your own needs.

If you are a passenger, respect your captain's system and try to pack the raft as he or she likes.

FRAMES

Oar frames come in all shapes and sizes. There are stern mount frames for rowing with paddlers on the sides, frames designed primarily for fishing, and frames set up to carry lots of cargo.

For multiday trips, you'll want a center mount frame that places the rower in the middle of the raft. With this setup you can have up to four paddlers—two in the front and two in the back—but really the center mount frame is most commonly used for solo rowers with nonpaddling passengers and gear.

That's not to say a stern mount frame cannot be used in this scenario. It can, but it does not provide infrastructure for storing gear, and for the raft with a stern mount frame to be balanced and maneuverable you need people in the bow for paddle support. The stern mount setup is useful if you plan to take inexperienced paddlers down a whitewater river where it can be hard for a paddle captain to maneuver the boat without the help of a talented crew.

Oar frames come in many configurations and sizes, as can be seen in this collection of rafts at the put-in for the Middle Fork River in Idaho.

Center-mounted frames put the rower at the pivot point of the boat, making it easy to spin the raft. It's hard to get that kind of control from the stern without paddlers up front to provide momentum and leverage.

Beyond the question of a stern or center mount, there are countless options to consider in choosing a frame. For most beginners, it's nice to start with a basic model. NRS makes modular frames that can be added to, adjusted, or manipulated as you gain experience and preferences. Fixed frames offer less flexibility, but if you plan to use your raft solely for multiday trips you will probably never need to make changes to your setup once you figure out what you like, so a fixed frame is fine as long as you know your needs. Breakdown frames are important for trips that you fly into or out from. Breakdown frames are also easier to transport. Some companies make custom frames that cater to your personal desires, but until you know what those desires are, it's nice to start with a basic, generic model.

If you are in the market for a frame, talk to your friends about what they are using on their rafts. Look at other setups you see on the river. Ask questions and try out different boats so that you begin to develop your own sense of what you like and dislike.

Many rafters personalize their oar frame setup, but the basic configuration has compartments for coolers and dry boxes, with gear loaded into the stern and/or bow compartments.

Frame size

To determine the correct frame size for your raft you need two measurements: the center-to-center measurement and the flat length measurement. To calculate the center-to-center size of your raft, measure its width and then subtract the width of one tube. To get the flat length measurement, measure the flat surface of the tube or pontoon to determine how long your frame can be. The flat surface is the level part of the tube between the two ends where the tubes turn up. If you are buying a standard frame, you can usually just tell dealers the size and model of your raft and they can steer you to the correct frame size.

You will see a lot of frames with built-in seats. For day trips, where you are not carrying coolers and dry boxes, you may need a seat so you have a place to sit to row. Seats are less common on multiday trips because they take up precious storage space, and some people find they actually interfere with their rowing motion. On multiday trips you generally see rowers sitting on padded dry boxes or coolers. For fishing, seats are nice because they allow you to pivot, and they get you a bit higher above the tubes for casting.

As for the actual configuration of your frame, there are many variations. The most basic frames for multiday whitewater trips have slots or compartments for dry boxes and coolers to rest in.

These rafts all have a basic frame setup, with the rower sitting on a padded dry box. A wooden beaver tail protects the floor in the stern of the raft in the foreground. The back raft has a cooler and two portable toilets in its stern.

OAR RETENTION SYSTEMS

Besides creating cargo space and a seat, the primary function of the frame is to provide a spot for your oars. The two most common oar retention systems are oarlocks and pins and clips. You'll hear some very vocal advocates of both of these systems, but like all systems where you have options, there are pros and cons to both.

Oarlocks

Oarlocks are the traditional technology used for holding oars in place. These are the classic U-shape metal hooks you see on almost all boats propelled by oars. The advantage of oarlocks is that they allow you to adjust the angle of the blade in the water, feather it through the air, and scull or skim the blade across the surface of the water. They also allow you to move the oar in and out laterally.

The open cup of the oarlock means your oar can pop out if it hits a rock with a lot of force (rather than break from the impact).

Oarlocks require **oar stops**, which are rubber donuts that slide or are bolted around the shaft about a third of the way down from the handle to prevent the

Traditional oarlocks have open, U-shape metal cups that allow you to rotate your oar to adjust the angle of the blade.

oar from slipping through the oarlock and into the river. Oar stops are usually used in conjunction with some kind of stopper sleeve or wrap that protects the shaft from wear.

The downside of oarlocks is that you must control the angle of the blade, which can be difficult in turbulent water. If the blade is at too steep of an angle to the water, it can dive down deeply and get pulled from your hand. Too shallow an angle and your blade may skip across the surface of the water. To help prevent either of these things from happening, some people use oars with oval-shaped grips so they can sense the position of the blade at all times by the feel of the grip in their hand; however, getting that feel takes practice and can be a challenge for beginner boaters.

Another way to avoid the angle problem is to use an **oar right.** An oar right holds the blade upright in the proper position for a full-powered stroke. The disadvantage to the oar right is that to change the angle of your blade or feather, you have to pull the oar in until the oar right is clear of the lock. For that reason most people who use oar rights do not bother to feather, which is fine because in reality most people don't bother to feather their blades anyway. Feathering puts a lot of stress on your wrists and elbows and can cause overuse injuries.

This image shows the oar stops, or rubber donuts, that encircle the oar shaft on top of a stopper sleeve to prevent the oar from slipping through the oarlock.

If you want the option of feathering, you can buy convertible oar rights that allow you to flip the spine that holds the oar in position up and out of the way, thus allowing you to feather between strokes when you desire.

An oar right, like the one pictured here, holds the blade upright in a vertical position with a plastic spine that runs between the sides of the oarlock.

Some people swear by oar rights, others swear about them. They can be a useful tool and give you added confidence in chaotic whitewater where you don't want to have to worry about whether your oar is positioned properly.

OAR LEASHES

Many boaters like to have leashes on their oars so they don't lose them if one gets knocked out by a rock or in the case of a flip. You can make your own tethers by tying a 4- to 5-foot piece of utility cord (3 millimeter Perlon accessory cord, or even parachute cord will suffice) to the frame near the oarlock with a bowline knot, and then tying it in a loop around the oar. Close that loop with another bowline knot.

The bowline is a versatile knot for rafters to know. It can be used to tie things off around a tree or post, and is easy to adjust by feeding slack through the system.

You can also buy ready-made leashes.

The only real downside to tethers is the entrapment hazard. To minimize this risk make your tethers as short as possible.

Pins and clips

The pin-and-clip method of oar retention entails a U-shape clip on the oar shaft that slips over a pin on the frame. The oar rotates around the pin with each stroke. The biggest advantage to the pin-and-clip system is that you always know the orientation of your blade, which is helpful in big whitewater where you may get tossed around and your oars deflected by rocks and powerful currents.

Pins and clips are safer to use with oar-assisted paddleboats than oarlocks because the oar always remains in place—held by a plastic retainer—even if it pops off the clip. That makes it less likely for a popped oar to clobber a passenger.

One disadvantage to pins and clips is that because the oars are fixed rigidly, they are more likely to break if you hit a rock. Finally, you cannot vary the angle of your blade with pins and clips.

Overall, pins and clips are most popular for big water and Class V rapids, where you don't want to worry about the angle of your blade and power is critical.

Both pins and clips and oarlocks work. If you don't already have a strong opinion based on your previous experience, try them both out to see which best suits your style.

OARS

Length

The best length oar for your raft is determined by the width of your raft and the physiology of the rower, as well as personal preference. People have different rowing styles and comfort zones as to where they like their hands. So, again, your best bet is to try out other people's rafts to get a sense of what length oar you find most comfortable.

That said, there are some general guidelines to help you determine the best average length if you don't have the luxury of doing a lot of testing. To determine this length, measure the distance between the two oarlocks on your raft frame. You are looking to have one third of your oar inside your oarlock and two thirds outside. Halve the distance between the two oarlocks to determine how long one-third of your oar should be then multiply that distance by three for the total oar length. This is a general rule of thumb, and you will probably find that your personal preference is slightly different, but it will give you a good place to start.

Rowers tend to have their own personal preferences for the right oar length. In general, you want your hands roughly in front of your shoulders for the most power.

Most manufacturers have tables to help you calculate the best oar length for your particular setup, but ultimately the best guideline is trial and error.

You want to be sure that the ends of your oar handles are at least a few inches apart to ensure you don't catch a hand between the oars in the heat of the moment.

Materials

Oars are made of everything from wood to fiberglass, carbon fiber, plastic, and aluminum. These materials affect the weight, flex, and feel of the oar as well as its cost. If you can, it's a good idea to try different oars to get a sense of how they feel. You may find you have a strong preference for one material over another. You may also find that your wallet dictates your choice.

TIP

If you are just starting out, buy a cheap set of oars to use until you figure out what you want in an oar. Once you are ready to upgrade, the old oars can become spares.

Oar material affects feel and flex.
STEFANIE VANDAELE

Oar Blades

Oar blades come in different shapes and sizes. For whitewater, a wide blade will give you the most power and versatility. For highly technical rivers, where you need precision over power, narrow blades are preferred. You can also find shoal-cut blades but these are designed specifically for shallow water and so are not recommended for an all-around river blade.

Paddles

Raft paddles also come in a variety of materials that affect their cost, feel, and durability. Read online reviews to help you sort through all the options, but if you are only paddling a few times a year you do not need a top-of-the-line paddle that will set you back a couple of hundred dollars.

Most raft paddlers use 60-inch paddles, although smaller paddlers may opt for shorter ones. You can get an idea of the best length by placing the paddle blade on the floor and seeing where it reaches on the paddler's body. The right length paddle should come up to your chin.

Guide paddlers typically go with a longer paddle—66 to 72 inches—so they get more leverage for steering.

INFLATING YOUR RAFT

The first step to setting up your raft is to inflate it. Because rafts can be unwieldy and awkward to move, it helps to place the raft close to the river so that when you unroll it downhill, the stern ends up at the water's edge and the bow is pointing uphill. This sets you up for moving off the beach once the raft is inflated, Of course, this point is moot if you have a trailer that allows you to transport your raft fully inflated.

Look at your valves. Some have a center-push spring that can be opened by pushing air into a closed valve or by using a finger to push, turn, and lock the valve open. Others require you to unscrew the valve by turning it counterclockwise to open.

To inflate your raft, open all the valves and pump air into the chambers in a clockwise direction, filling each to about 70 percent of its capacity. You want the raft to take shape but still be soft. Next, go around in a counterclockwise direction and fill each chamber to capacity, which will be a maximum of between 2 and 3 pounds per square inch (psi). If you don't have a pressure gauge, the psi number isn't that useful. Instead you'll go by feel. You want your raft to be firm but not taut. Press your knee into one of tubes. If this pressure causes the tube to crease, you probably need more air.

Using an electric pump off your car battery to inflate your raft helps speed up the inflation process.

Once the tubes are filled, inflate your floor. Many rafters recommend running with a slightly soft floor for better tracking. A hard floor tends to surf waves and holes, making the rafts more prone to flipping. Inflate the floor until the pressure relief valve exhausts a small amount of air. Most floors will hold about 2.5 psi.

After the main chambers are inflated, inflate the thwarts if you have them. Again, inflate each to about 70 percent and then go back and top them off until they are firm (about 2 to 2.5 psi).

A properly inflated raft will have some give to the tubes without being too soft.

As air temperature and atmospheric pressure change, your raft's tube pressure will change. It may be soft in the morning after a cold night; or rock hard after sitting out in the hot sun. The pressure can also change if you tow an inflated raft on a trailer to the river, so be sure to check it periodically en route.

Today's high-quality rafts can withstand a great deal of pressure on their seams, but overinflation strains them, and in extreme cases a raft could blow out its seams. Also, overinflated rafts are more prone to punctures, so it's important

Air temperature will affect your raft's tube pressure. You may find you need to top off the tubes in the morning after a cool night or let air out during hot, sunny days.

PUMPS

AC electric pumps blow up your raft quickly, and many popular river put-ins have 110-volt outlets to accommodate them, but check before you assume you'll be able to plug in. A DC electric pump that runs off your car battery also works for inflating your raft at a put-in. There is a wide range of price points for pumps. If you opt for a cheaper model, beware. They tend to overheat, which can blow out the motor.

Once you are on the river, you'll need a foot or hand pump to top off the tubes. For hand pumps you have two basic configurations to choose from: a 6-inch barrel pump and a 4-inch barrel pump. The 4-inch model is best for topping your raft off.

The range in price for foot or hand pumps is pretty wide. Make sure the pump you purchase can provide adequate pressure to inflate your raft. A pump designed for a stand-up paddleboard (SUP) or an inflatable kayak is not adequate for a 16-foot raft. If in doubt, ask a salesperson what type of pump you need.

to let air out of the tubes if the raft gets too hard. For a rock–hard raft, get four people on each of the tube valves to ensure you release air at the same time in all the tubes or, if you don't have four people, release air from each tube in very small bursts. You can cause a baffle to blow out if you let too much air out of one chamber when another is still overinflated.

A soft raft, on the other hand, tends to be sluggish and unresponsive in whitewater, so if your raft feels mushy, add some air. The only time you want soft tubes is when the water is low and the river rocky. In that case, soft tubes tend to ooze over rocks rather than get stuck, which is advantageous when you can't avoid them.

To deflate your raft, open all the valves starting with the thwarts and floor, and then work around the tubes, beginning at the one you filled last. You can lie on the tubes to help force air out. When the raft is flat, roll or fold it for transporting.

RIGGING YOUR OAR RIG

It's a good idea to strap your frame onto your raft before it is fully inflated. Follow the steps for inflating your raft, but stop when it is about 90 percent full. Then pick up your frame and place it so it is centered in the middle of the raft.

For most conventional frames, there will be one space in the front for a dry box or rocket boxes, a cockpit, and then one or two storage spaces in the stern. Make sure the frame is centered side to side as well as front to back. Some

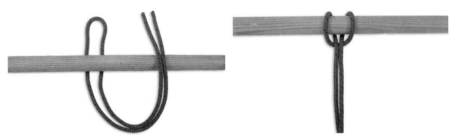

A girth hitch is a simple way to attach straps to the frame. Fold a bight of cord around the frame and then feed the ends through it and cinch down.

people like to push the frame slightly forward of center to get more weight in the bow of the raft when they anticipate big water (we're talking a few inches only). Weight in the front helps rafts plow through big waves.

Girth hitch 2-foot, 1.5-inch-wide cam straps to the D rings, with the cam buckle close to the D ring, facing right side up, so the strap can be tightened with an upward pull from on the boat. Some frames come with frame straps in place, or you can leave the straps you add permanently. This makes rigging easier in the future. Strap down the four corners of the frame. Avoid twists in the lash straps, and just snug things down gently at first. You'll tighten the straps later.

Some straps come with sewn loops for girth-hitching around the raft frame.

Center your frame on your raft and then strap it in place by girth hitching 2-foot cam straps at each corner on a D ring.

Attach another 2-foot strap to the D ring in front of each of the oarlock fittings. Check to make sure everything is centered and the frame is secured at all attachment points.

Place the boat in the water. The pressure in the raft chambers will decrease from contact with the cold water. Let it sit for about ten minutes, then pump up the raft until it is at 100 percent capacity, adding air evenly to all sections. Once your boat is firm, tighten down the lash straps so the frame is securely in place.

Check that the oarlocks are secure. You'll want to do this periodically during your trip as they can loosen with use.

Lash a spare oar (or two) on the outside of the frame. Don't cinch the straps down too tightly as that can cause the oar to break when the boat flexes in big waves.

For safety, it's important to carry at least one spare oar on each raft. Lash the oar to the frame loosely so it won't break when the raft flexes in big waves.

KEEPING DRY BOXES OFF THE FLOOR

Dry boxes should be suspended from the frame to protect the floor of your raft. You can create a sling with lash straps to hold your boxes up, or you can slide your boxes into mesh bags that some companies manufacture to keep them up off the floor. Better yet, you can weld aluminum wedges onto your dry box, or buy a dry box with these wedges already in place. The wedges sit on top of the frame and keep your dry boxes off the floor.

Many rafters like to have a wooden or metal floor in their boats. You can have a floor in your cockpit, as well as a so-called "beaver tail" floor in the bow and/or stern. These floors are usually custom-made and are suspended from the raft by lash straps. The advantage of a floor is that it gives you something firm to stand or walk on and, more importantly, it keeps gear off the bottom of your raft, protecting the floor from sharp objects that can cause punctures.

You can also buy mesh beaver tails for your cargo holds. Mesh floors tend to be less effective at suspending your gear than a wooden or metal beaver tail, but they are cheap.

Once your floors are in, it's time to load your dry boxes and coolers, unless you are heading out for a day trip and don't need storage. Then these things can stay at home. Still it's likely you'll need something to sit on if your raft doesn't have a seat, so you'll need at least one box in your frame.

Most oar frames have compartments to slide dry boxes and coolers into so they are secure in the raft and suspended off the floor.

LASH STRAPS

Lots of companies make lash straps, but the industry standard is NRS's 1-inch, HD (heavy-duty) tie-down straps. NRS's straps are rated up to 1,500 pounds so you don't have to worry about losing your gear, and the cam buckle grips securely so you won't have any slippage even if you flip. If you opt to use another brand of lash strap, make sure it meets these criteria.

Lash straps come in assorted lengths, ranging from 2-footers to 20-footers, as well as loop straps. You'll need an assortment of straps to lash down your gear. Nowadays, you can buy straps that are color-coded by length, which speeds up your rigging as you don't have to dig around looking for the number indicating strap length. Remember to write your name with a permanent marker on the strap or cam buckle. You can also spray paint the buckle an identifiable color so you recognize your straps. It's easy to mix up straps on a big expedition.

You always want to strap your gear into your raft securely in case of an unanticipated flip. Straps with cam buckles, like the NRS HD straps in use here, allow you to tighten down the load so it stays in place.

To be prepared, you should always rig to flip, which means strapping everything in. I've seen a raft get hung up on rocks in a flat section of river, where enough water flooded into the boat to float the gear, so even when you are planning a mellow day on the river, get into the habit of lashing things down.

It's nice to have "loop straps" for lashing down boxes and coolers. Loop straps have loops on one end that can be girth hitched onto the frame. The other end of the straps will have either a cam buckle or a tailpiece that feeds through the cam buckle.

For lashing down boxes, 4- or 6-foot loop straps are adequate. Orient your straps so that you are pulling away from the frame to tighten the strap, and make sure all cam buckles face the same way so it's easy to cinch things down.

LOADING GEAR ONTO YOUR PADDLE RAFT

When you carry gear on a paddle raft it is usually loaded into the central cockpit between the thwarts. This gives paddlers room at either end of the raft to paddle. Again, it's a good idea to suspend a floor off the D rings to keep your cargo off the bottom of the raft. Depending on the size of the raft and the number of people on your trip, you can usually fit a cooler and/or a small dry box, together with dry bags for camping equipment and food. It's very doable—think how small your backpack is—but you have to be thoughtful in the equipment you choose to bring along. And you may want to load up the raft at home first to make sure you have space for everything you need.

Once the gear is in place, lash it down, taking care to run straps through everything to ensure it stays in place.

OTHER ESSENTIAL RIVER GEAR

We'll go into detail about camping gear later, but for now you need a few more things before you are ready to hit the water.

Personal Flotation Devices (PFDs)

PFDs are an essential part of your river-running gear. All members of your group should wear one whenever they are on the water.

Most adults need at least 12 pounds of flotation to keep their heads above water. For whitewater, the recommended minimum is 15.5 pounds. PFDs with lower flotation are usually less bulky and more comfortable, but whitewater tends to be aerated and provides less support than flat water, making added

Failure to wear a PFD is one of the leading causes of river fatalities. All members of your team should wear a properly fitting, Coast Guard–approved PFD whenever they are on the water.

flotation more critical. For big water, many rafters opt for vests with as much as 25 pounds of flotation to help keep them afloat should they take a swim.

The US Coast Guard rates personal flotation devices or lifejackets according to their intended use and minimum buoyancy. The more buoyant the vest, the bulkier it will be.

Most whitewater rafters opt for Type III PFDs, although commercial river trips may require passengers to wear Type II or Type V lifejackets designed for whitewater. Some rivers have restrictions on the type of PFD you can use, so it's worth confirming that you are OK with a Type III vest before launching. All PFDs should be Coast Guard–approved. Also, if your PFD is faded, if the writing has worn off, or if it has holes or damage, it's time to retire it. Your PFD is your lifesaver. Don't use one that is worn out.

US COAST GUARD LIFEJACKET CLASSIFICATIONS

- Type I lifejackets have a minimum of 22 pounds of flotation and are designed for extended survival in rough water far from shore.
- Type II lifejackets are the classic lifejacket. They have a minimum of 15.5 pounds of flotation and are intended for use on inland waterways where rescue is usually quick. Most Type II PFDs are designed to turn an unconscious person face up.
- Type III lifejackets are generally the most comfortable and sleekest. Designed for use during sports like paddling or water skiing, Type III PFDs provide a minimum of 15.5 pounds of flotation. They will not turn an unconscious person face up.
- Type V flotation devices are designed for special uses. Many provide up to 22 pounds of flotation, so are good for big water. Type V PFDs should only be used for the specific purpose for which they are intended. That use is printed inside the vest. Rescue vests, which include a built-in releasable tow system, are Type V vests. You may also find Type V PFDs with a pillow behind the head that is designed to turn swimmers onto their backs. These PFDs are recommended in big whitewater.

Your PFD must be snug, yet still allow you to move freely. Features such as multiple adjustment points, large armholes, and short waists enable you to get a good fit and allow you to row or paddle comfortably without chafing. You can narrow down your options by measuring the circumference of your chest to figure out your size. (Kids' sizes are determined by weight.) Many manufacturers make vests specially designed for women, which may provide a better fit than a unisex version, especially for women with large chests.

For people whose stomachs are bigger than their chests, you should add a strap that runs between their legs and attaches to the vest to keep it from sliding up over their heads if they end up in the water.

The best bet for ensuring you'll be comfortable in your PFD all day on the river is to go to a boating store and try on different models to see what fits best.

To try out a PFD, loosen all the straps, put the vest on, and zip it up—or pull it over your head if it's a pullover. Starting at the waist, tighten down all the straps. The vest should feel snug but not tight. If you feel something rubbing or if the straps cut into your neck at this point, it's not the right model for you. Have someone try to lift you by pulling up on the PFD's shoulder straps. If the vest moves up past your nose, tighten the straps further and try again. If it still comes up over your head the PFD is too large.

PFDs must be snug but allow you to move freely, with enough flotation to keep you afloat.

To ensure your PFD fits properly, have someone lift you up by the shoulder straps. If the vest comes up over your face, it's too big.

RESCUE VESTS

Rescue vests are designed to provide buoyancy and freedom of movement for paddling whitewater, as well as to be used for rescues. The main difference between a rescue vest and a Type III PFD is that a rescue vest includes a built-in quick-release harness belt system (QRHS). Rescue vests also tend to have less flotation than other types.

A rescue vest is a tool with limitations, and requires training and consistent practice to use safely and effectively. If you intend to boat hard whitewater, you should probably wear and know how to use a rescue vest, but don't spent money on an expensive rescue vest unless you plan to learn how to use it.

Move your arms around, and twist and turn as if you are rowing or paddling, to make sure there are no places where the PFD chafes or restricts movement.

If you try all these things and the PFD feels like a comfortable extra skin, you've found your match.

You may also want to consider the following when selecting your PFD:

- Bright colors and reflective tape make you easier to see if you come out of your raft and are floating downstream.
- Pockets are helpful for carrying lip balm, sunscreen or a snack.
- Attachment points are useful for securing a knife or whistle to the outside of the jacket.

Helmets

According to American Whitewater's Safety Code, you should wear a helmet when "upsets are likely." That guideline is a bit vague and definitely open to interpretation. Clearly, helmets are essential in whitewater kayaks where it's common to flip and be left hanging upside down, exposing your head to underwater rocks until you roll up or come out of your boat. Rafts are a bit different. It's not common to flip a raft, although it certainly happens. However, it is common to get ejected from one and end up swimming through rapids where you are vulnerable to head injuries. It's also common to get clobbered by an errant oar or paddle. Despite this you often see rafters descending whitewater without helmets.

In moving water or mellow whitewater (Class II), it's easy for most people to keep their heads above water and avoid clocking their noggins on rocks. But when you start swimming Class III and above, it becomes increasingly difficult

Rafters don't always wear helmets, but if you are running rapids where there's a chance you might fall out of the boat or flip your raft, wearing one to protect your head is a good idea.

to control your movements. Most of the time you are at the mercy of the river and will have to fight hard to avoid rocks and obstacles. If you fall on a raft going through a rapid, you can hit your head on things like ammo cans or oarlocks. If your raft flips, those objects become even more dangerous. For all these reasons, wearing a helmet in whitewater is smart.

Ultimately, you need to decide if you want to wear a helmet, as most river regulations do not require their use. Remember, helmets are never a bad idea, especially on rocky, technical rivers with steep drops and long rapids. You should wear one whenever you run challenging whitewater.

One of the key factors in finding the right helmet is comfort. If your helmet is uncomfortable you are less likely to wear it, so make sure you find one that fits well. The best helmets are light, strong, and sit snugly on your head, but aren't so tight you end up with a headache after a few hours in your boat. Your helmet should have a chinstrap that is secured with a quick-release buckle. Remember, the helmet only works if that strap is closed.

Carbon helmets are lightweight, but can cost a couple of hundred dollars. Plastic or fiberglass helmets may be slightly heavier, but they tend to cost less than $100 and are perfectly adequate. Go to a whitewater boating store and try on a few models to see what you like best.

Occasionally you will see people wearing bike or climbing helmets on a river. If you have nothing else, I guess these helmets are OK, but they are designed for different impacts and are really not great for whitewater. If you plan to be a boater, buy yourself a helmet meant for whitewater.

Clothing

What you wear in the boat will be determined by the ambient air and water temperatures. The American Canoeing Association (ACA) defines cold-water conditions as any water that is less than 60 degrees Fahrenheit, or when the combined air and water temperature is less than 120 degrees Fahrenheit. In these conditions, swimmers rapidly lose their ability to function as they succumb to the cold and become hypothermic.

If you plan to raft in cold-water conditions, you need to dress accordingly. This can be a wet suit, a dry suit, a paddling jacket, and/or rain gear. Your choice

Hypothermia can be life-threatening. If you are boating in cold water or cool temperatures, you need to dress warmly. This rafter is wearing a dry suit.

will be determined by the nature of the river you are running, your activity level, and the weather conditions. If a swim is likely, go with a wet or dry suit. If you are just going to get splashed or rained on, a paddling jacket and pants, or waterproof rain gear will suffice. If you are rowing or paddling, you'll need less warmth. If you are a passenger, bundle up. You may also need hats, gloves, and warm waterproof shoes if conditions are really chilly. The key is to stay safe and comfortable. It's always easier to cool off with a swim if you get hot than it is to warm up when you get cold. We'll go into more detail on specifics later in the book.

In warm weather or warm water, you don't need to be as concerned about hypothermia. Often a bathing suit and shorts will suffice in terms of temperature control. But you do need to be careful about sun protection. Many rafters opt to wear a long-sleeved cotton shirt to block out the sun. A hat with a big brim and a cord that can be tightened under the chin or behind the nape of the neck to keep it in place is also helpful. You may opt to wear a Buff or bandanna pulled up over your face and cotton gloves on your hands if the sun's glare is really intense. In mellow water, people often rig sunshades to provide some relief, and you can always jump into the river to cool off if the temperatures soar too high.

We'll go into more detail about what to wear in your boat in Chapter Seven: Personal Camping Gear.

In hot weather, a wide-brimmed hat and sun shirt can help you stay cool and avoid sunburn. Plus, you can always jump in the water to cool down.

Throw bags and safety equipment

We will go into detail about safety equipment in Chapter Thirteen, which covers basic river rescue. Just know that before you hit the river with your raft you need to have a throw rope or throw bag on board, and you need to know how to use it. Most rafters clip their throw ropes on the raft in a place where they can get to it quickly. If they are rowing, it will be on the frame in the cockpit near where they sit. If they are guiding a paddle raft, the throw bag is usually clipped to a D ring in the stern.

Some raft guides like to carry a throw rope around the waist as well as have one clipped onto the raft.

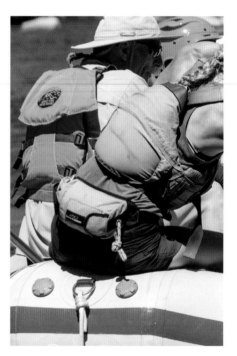

Many rafters carry throw bags clipped around their waists for immediate access if someone goes for an accidental swim.

Throw ropes typically come in either 55- or 75-foot lengths. On big rivers and with rafts, the longer lengths are recommended. Choose a throw rope that comes in a roomy stuff sack. You want to be able to get the rope in and out of the bag quickly and easily, and if it's a tight fit that can be difficult.

Throw ropes are made from a variety of materials that affect weight, strength, and cost. All are designed to float on the surface of the water. The cheapest ropes are made from polypropylene, but polypro isn't as strong as some of the other

Roomy storage sacks make stuffing your throw bag between uses easier and faster.

materials such as Spectra, so if you plan to do a lot of rafting it may be worth considering a sturdier rope that can be used for rescue.

You should also consider carrying a river knife to cut yourself out of ropes or other entanglements, and a whistle to alert your team in an emergency.

Most rafters carry a whistle and a river knife on their PFDs for emergencies.

CHAPTER THREE
RAFTING SKILLS

Once your raft is ready for the water, it's time to get out there to practice your rowing and paddling techniques. Start on an easy river to gain confidence and skill. Look for rivers with a good current, well-developed eddies—calm spots below obstacles or changes in the river bank—and a few easy obstacles to navigate around as you gain comfort moving downstream. If you have a more experienced buddy, bring him or her along to coach you. Make sure your chosen river does not have any must-make moves or high hazards. You don't want a waterfall or dam downstream of a hard-to-make takeout on your first adventure on the water.

PADDLE RAFTS

Seating arrangement

Your seating arrangement depends on the number of people and size of your raft. Your goal is to distribute strength evenly around the boat, give everyone plenty of room to paddle, and make sure the weight is evened out.

In general, you want your most powerful and experienced paddlers in the bow. They need to be able to set an even paddling pace that others can follow and be willing to paddle hard into the face of an upcoming rapid. They also need to be able to listen and respond quickly to commands from the captain.

Paddle captains usually sit in the stern of the raft, where they can watch their teams and the upcoming rapids, shout out commands, and exert a powerful rudder or draw stroke to determines the raft's direction of travel. Usually the stern compartment is the raft captain's private domain so he or she has plenty of room to maneuver and oversee the rest of the boat.

Distribute your paddlers evenly along the tubes, starting to fill up the raft from the front and working back toward the stern. The role of the middle paddlers is to follow the bow paddlers' lead and pull hard.

Paddle rafts are steered by a captain who sits in the rear of the raft. Paddlers sit on the tubes along the sides with the bravest, strongest paddlers in front.

Position

A powerful paddle stroke requires a strong foundation against which paddlers can brace their bodies. Some paddle rafts come with foot cups on the floor, but if yours does not, you can achieve the same strong position by sitting on the raft tubes and bracing your feet and shins against the tube and thwart. Don't wedge your foot all the way under a tube as it can get stuck and be an entrapment hazard if your raft flips. Sit with both legs inside the raft and your buttocks far enough out on the tube to allow you to reach into the water for a stroke but not so far out that you'll fall off the raft at the first wave.

If it's your first time paddling, practice in a few different positions to figure out where you are most stable. You can even have someone push you around a bit to see if you are secure. You don't have to be in this position at all times. In flat water it's fine to relax and even dangle your legs around the tube, but when

Paddlers need to be in a strong, braced position to withstand the impact of whitewater and to have a powerful, effective stroke.

the water starts moving and there are rocks around, it's dangerous to have a leg outside the raft

To execute a strong, effective stroke you need to use your entire body. Lean forward to catch the water with your blade. Tighten your stomach muscles and brace your legs against the thwart and tubes and so you can use them and your back as well as your arms to move the blade through the water. Rest and relax on the recovery.

Paddle grip

Good paddling technique includes a good grip. Paddles come with some form of T-shaped handle at the end of the shaft. The handle is designed to let your fingers wrap around the top of the grip while your thumb comes up around the bottom. This grip allows you to control the angle of your blade and lessens the chance that you'll drop the paddle.

Your bottom hand clasps the shaft with the palm facing forward about two-thirds of the way down from the handle. Your hands should be closed around the paddle, but you don't need a death grip. Relax your fingers to prevent fatigue.

Holding the paddle improperly can be hazardous. A common raft guide joke warns clients of "summer-mouth teeth," which happens when someone hasn't gripped the top of the T-grip properly and ends up clobbering a buddy in the face, leaving "sum" teeth in his mouth and "sum" in the bottom of the raft. You can avoid that problem by always keeping your fingers folded over the top of the grip with your thumb coming up from the bottom.

You'll find you have a natural preference for one side or the other. If you plan to do a lot of whitewater paddle rafting, it's a good idea to learn to paddle on both sides of the raft so you are more versatile.

Forward stroke

For most paddle rafters, the forward stroke is going to be the stroke you use 90 percent of the time. It's a fairly natural stroke, but good technique enhances its effectiveness and helps prevent fatigue and overuse injuries, so it's worth taking some time to master the basics.

Start by leaning forward and reaching ahead into the water with your blade. To make this reach, rotate at the waist and thrust your outside shoulder toward the bow to wind up your torso. Lean your body forward about 10 degrees to maximize your extension. Your lower arm should be straight and your upper arm slightly bent and held around eye level, with the blade at a 90-degree angle to the tube.

Plant the blade into the water next to the raft tube for the catch. The paddle should be at about a 70-degree angle to the water's surface.

Now unwind your torso, pulling back with your lower arm and pushing with your upper. This rotation should provide the power to your stroke rather than your arms. Try to keep the paddle blade close to vertical.

Most of your power will come in the first few inches of the stroke, diminishing as you get closer to your hip. When you really need power, take short, fast strokes and never pull your paddle past your hip.

Finish the stroke just in front of your hip, pulling the blade out of the water by rotating your wrist slightly and lifting the blade up. Reach forward for your next stroke and repeat.

HINTS FOR A MORE POWERFUL FORWARD STROKE

- Imagine you are planting your blade in cement and pulling your body and the raft past it rather than pulling your blade toward you.
- Concentrate on your torso rotation.
- Don't let your upper hand get too high; keep it at eye level or lower.
- Time your strokes so you dig into water, not the air between waves or the froth of a hole. Reach ahead and look for dark water.
- Make sure your paddle is the proper length so you can sink three-quarters of the blade into the water for the most power.

For a strong forward stroke, rotate at the waist to engage your entire body rather than just your arms. Short, quick strokes are more efficient and effective than long strokes.

Back paddle

The back paddle is basically just the reverse of a forward stroke. For the catch, you'll rotate your outside shoulder back toward the stern, planting the blade in the water slightly behind your hip. As you move the blade through the water, rotate at the waist to bring your outside shoulder forward until the blade is just in front of your hip. Twist the blade out of the water and rotate back to your starting point.

The big challenge with the back paddle is that you are fighting the momentum of the raft and the current. Often you'll see paddlers just plant the paddle in place and lean against the current rather than finish the stroke. You can use your body as a fulcrum, placing the paddle shaft against your outside hip to give you some leverage to move the paddle forward. This technique gives you power and supports your shoulder. However, be careful. If your blade hits a rock or a strong hydraulic, you can be pole-vaulted out of the raft before you know what is happening.

Draw stroke

Draw strokes are used to move the raft sideways, allowing you to pull into a dock, up to another boat, or away from an obstacle.

To perform a draw stroke, place the paddle vertically into the water about 2 feet from the side of the raft with the blade facing the raft and the shaft at a slight angle from the water to your upper hand. To get this reach, you'll need to twist your torso so your outside shoulder is pointing toward the stern of the raft and the inside shoulder is pointing toward the bow. The blade enters the water around your hip and should be fully immersed. Your upper hand should be close to your head. It will serve as a pivot point for the paddle.

Pull the blade toward you with your lower hand, straightening the shaft until your upper hand is above your lower one. Be careful not to bring the blade all the way into the boat.

At this point you can lift the blade out of the water and move it back out to the starting point for another stroke. Alternatively, once you can have drawn the blade in toward the boat, slide it forward or back in the water to initiate some other stroke.

Practice having one side of the boat perform simultaneous draw strokes. Effective teams can "slip" their rafts sideways to avoid obstacles with this technique.

Turning strokes

The easiest way to turn a raft is for the paddlers on one side to paddle forward while those on the other side paddle backward. This method changes the direction of the raft swiftly, but it also slows down its momentum by putting on the brakes on one side. The boat will turn toward the side of the back-paddling paddlers.

You can also "spin" the raft using a combination of draw and pry strokes (see below) in the bow and stern. Play around with your crew to see how these work.

Captaining

The captain of a paddle raft typically sits in the stern and uses a longer paddle that enables him or her to control the boat. The captain does all the normal paddle strokes—forward, reverse—but he or she also employs a pry or draw stroke for quick changes in direction. These strokes can be used in other positions in the raft, but that typically involves a skilled, practiced team. With more novice paddlers, it's usually just the captain who employs a pry or draw.

Draw strokes in the stern are the same as described above. The only real difference is that paddle captains use them more commonly than their crews. From the stern, the captain reaches out and away from the raft and then pulls the paddle in, creating a powerful turning motion. A draw stroke in the stern turns the boat away from the side it is performed on.

Pry strokes, which are also called rudders, turn the bow toward the side that it is performed on. A pry on the right turns the boat right, and vice versa,

To perform a pry or rudder, rotate your shoulders so they are parallel to the raft tube. Reach back and place the paddle in the water roughly 8 inches behind the hip. The lower arm should be bent, while the upper arm is nearly straight and at a 90-degree angle to the centerline of the raft. Place the shaft of the paddle on either the raft tube or your thigh to act as a pivot point.

The paddle captain's role is to steer the raft and shout out commands to the crew. On flat water this is easy. In rapids it gets more demanding.

The blade is set in the water so it is parallel to the raft tube. Pull your upper hand in, levering the blade against the pivot point. You only get a few inches of real power before you lose your leverage, so pry strokes should be short and quick.

Commands

Besides steering, the captain's role is to get his or her crew working in unison. Put your most experienced and skilled paddlers in the bow of the raft so the people in the middle can follow them. The bow paddlers need to be the ones who are most likely and able to follow your commands. Things get exciting and chaotic quickly in a rapid, especially with newer paddlers, so practice going through your commands with them on flat water before your trip starts rocking.

Most of the time your commands are going to be pretty straightforward. You either want your paddlers to be paddling forward, backward, or resting. Make sure everyone knows which side of the raft they are on. Knowing right from left is important! Your directions will be set by the orientation of the raft moving downstream, with the bow in the front. Paddlers on the right side in this orientation will always be considered to be on the right side, even if you are heading downstream backward.

It helps to call out the number of strokes you want your paddlers to perform. Open-ended instructions, such as "paddle forward," often end up with the paddlers tapering off after a while, whereas a specific number keeps their attention.

In addition, paddlers should know what it means when the captain says "High side." Basically, this command tells everyone to move to the high side of the boat to try to bounce off an obstacle.

Paddle commands
- All forward, four strokes (or whatever number you determine is needed)
- Left forward, include number of strokes
- Right forward, include number of strokes
- All back, include number of strokes
- Left back, right back
- Right draw, left draw
- High side
- Rest or stop

You may also find yourself needing to call for more power—hard right, hard left, or "dig in," etc.. If one side is constantly overpowering the other, you may have to call for that side to lighten up.

Captains are most effective if they give these commands in a loud, calm voice. Screaming frantically gets everyone on edge and is usually counterproductive. Be consistent. It doesn't matter if you choose to say "stop" or "rest," but it helps to use the same word every time so your crew responds immediately.

If you are heading out with a crew of novice paddlers, take time to perform some maneuvers in the flat water above the rapids so your crew gets a sense of how the boat responds and what it's like to work together. Practice spinning the raft in both directions and experiment with different strokes in a calm, controlled setting, so when things get a bit crazy in the rapids your crew will know what to do.

Ferrying

Ferrying is the act of moving your raft from one side of the river to the other with minimal downstream drift. To perform a ferry you paddle or row against the current, using its power to push your raft across. The keys to an effective ferry are angle and speed, and the proper angle and speed are determined by the river's velocity.

Your raft should be placed anywhere from 30 to 90 degrees to the current. If you find you are being carried downstream, close up your angle to closer to 30 degrees. If you are fighting the current and staying in place, make the angle wider so you'll move across the river.

FERRY TERMS

- **Angle:** Angle describes the vector angle of the raft relative to the current.
- **Front ferry:** In a front ferry, the paddlers or rowers face upstream and forward paddle or push at an angle against the current.
- **Back or upstream ferry:** In a back or upstream ferry, the paddlers or rower face downstream and back-paddle or pull at an angle against the current.
- **Downstream ferry:** A true ferry is always against the current, but rafters use the term loosely and employ the moniker "downstream ferry" to describe when they row or paddle downstream at an angle to, and faster than or with, the current. This is not a true ferry, but it is an effective way to maintain momentum and use the current to help you move your boat in different directions.

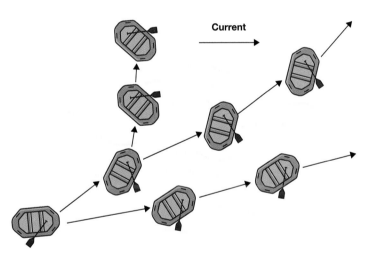

A ferry uses the force of the current to move the raft across the river. In this diagram, the left raft is performing a classic upstream ferry. The raft is about 30 degrees to the current and the paddlers would be forward paddling. The second raft is doing what is known as a downstream ferry. The boat is angled and the paddlers would be forward paddling with the current to cross the river. The third raft is just moving downstream.
AVERY ABSOLON

OAR RIGS

Unlike captaining a paddle raft, when you get behind the oars in a raft you are usually on your own. Rowing is very different from paddling. You are basically limited to pulling or pushing your oars back and forth to maneuver and power your craft downstream.

Pulling

The standard rowing stroke—used in crew shells and rowboats— is the pulling stroke. This stroke has more power than a pushing stroke, but there is one obvious disadvantage: It can be harder to see what you are moving toward.

Newer rowers commonly pull too much. Pulling expends more energy than pushing and causes you to work against the river rather than with it. Pulling is an important stroke to know, but don't over use it.

When rafters pull, they tend to float downstream at an angle that allows them to keep an eye out for what is coming so they can ferry away from the obstacle or quickly spin into a power position to pull away. It helps to pick a landmark upstream to focus on so you stay straight as you move backward.

The pulling stroke is most effective when you use your core and legs as well as your arms to exert force on the oars. To do this, brace your feet against something so you can push off with your legs as you move the oars through the water.

To initiate the pulling stroke, push down on the oar grips so the blades are above the water, lean forward at the waist, reaching out straight ahead with your arms. When you are at full reach, lift your hands to drop the oars into the water for the **catch**. When your blade is fully submerged, push back against your feet and tighten your abdominal muscles while you sit up, moving your shoulders back to your starting position. This is the **power** stage of the stroke.

When your body is vertical, bend your arms, pulling the oars in toward your chest to finish the stroke. As with paddle strokes, the finish of the pulling stroke is its weakest point, so it's a waste of time and energy to lean way back to eke out a few more inches of pull. Furthermore, you expose your ribcage to the oar handle in this position, which can lead to a broken rib if your oar hits a rock.

When you get to the end of the stroke, push your hands down to lift the blades out of the water and reach forward for your next stroke. This is called the **recovery** phase. If you are feathering your blades between strokes, roll your knuckles forward until they face down to rotate the blades so they are parallel to the water's surface. You'll roll your knuckles back so the blades are vertical before you drop them in the water for your next stroke. Often rowers will only feather their oars in high winds. The repeated wrist curl can lead to tendonitis.

Make sure to use your entire body rather than just the muscles in your lower back and arms during each stroke. Try to exert equal pressure on the oars. Most of us have a weaker side, so you may find you have to correct by taking an extra stroke on the weak side every now and then to straighten the raft out.

To help you stay straight when rowing backward down river, pick a point on the horizon that lines up with your desired direction and use it as a guide. Make sure to check over your shoulder now and again to ensure you are on the right track.

A rower's strongest stroke is the pulling or rowing stroke. These photos show one stroke from the catch, where the oars are dropped into the water, through the finish, where the rower is ready to take another stroke.

WATCH OUT FOR THESE COMMON ROWING ERRORS

Below are a few common errors that affect your stroke's efficiency, and that can cause injuries over time. With a little practice and awareness they are easy to avoid.

- *Overreaching at the catch.* If you lean too far forward before you put your oar into the water, you stress your lower back. Furthermore, your stroke is weakest at its extreme ends. You are better off taking shorter strokes and protecting your back by limiting your forward reach.
- *Leaning too far back at the finish.* Some people lean way back before they lift their oars out of the water. You don't gain any power from this lean, and you do make your lower back vulnerable to strain. You should have only a slight backward lean—say 10 degrees or so—at the finish of your stroke.
- *Pressing your hands down too far on the recovery and lunging at the catch.* As you move your hands forward in the recovery phase, avoid pushing down on the oar handles, which will cause the blades to lift up too high. Your goal is to move your hands forward on an even plane so the blades stay level just above the water. Take care to maintain this level movement as you approach the catch as well. Some people tend to lunge forward at the end of the recovery, which causes their hands to dive and the blades to shoot up before they drop into the water.
- *Chicken-wing arms.* On the recovery try to keep your elbows close to the side of your body and your shoulders low. This helps you conserve energy during the stroke.
- *Rowing with just your arms.* For a powerful stroke you need to use your entire body, especially the big strong muscles in your legs and back. To access these muscles, brace your feet and tighten your core as you set your blade in the water.
- *Digging too deeply.* If you raise your hands too high in the power phase of the stroke, your oar blades will plunge down deeply, often hitting the rocks or the bottom of the river. You may feel as if you are getting more power by digging deeply, but actually you are more efficient and stronger if you maintain an even pull higher in the water column. If you need more power, increase the cadence of your stroke rather than lowering your blades.

Pushing stroke or portegee

The pushing stroke or portegee is the opposite of rowing. Instead of pulling the oars toward your body, you push them away to move the boat forward. The advantage to pushing rather than pulling is that you face downstream and, therefore, can watch for hazards and obstacles coming toward you. Plus, you use the current to help you move. But pushing is not as powerful as pulling, so it takes skill, practice, and a bit of finesse to push rather than pull your way through a rapid.

Begin the pushing stroke by lowering your hands until the oar blades are out of the water and bringing them in toward your belly. Raise your hands and drop the blades into the water. This is the **catch**. Your blades should project straight out from the raft at your sides.

Bend forward at the waist and simultaneously push the oar handles forward to move the oars through the water, keeping your hands about level. For added power, many rowers drop their heads slightly at the end of the stroke, causing their arms and shoulders to rise slightly, but it's a subtle movement. If you lift your hands too high the blade will dive down too deeply. Brace your feet so you can engage your legs and back as you push. This is the **power** phase of the stroke.

When your arms are straight in front of you (keep your elbows soft), push down on the handles of the oars to lift the blades out of the water and repeat the cycle.

This series of photos shows a rower pushing his oars through the water to move downstream. Notice how he engages his entire body for power and to help conserve his arm strength.

CONSERVING ENERGY

If you decide to push in flat-water sections of the river, you can vary the stroke to conserve energy by pushing one oar through the water at a time, alternating from side to side. Standing up to push is also a handy trick, especially above a rapid because it allows you to see what lies ahead.

You can conserve energy by varying your stroke as you move downstream. One trick is to alternate arms.

Turning

The fastest way to turn your boat is to push with one oar and pull with the other to spin the raft. The raft will rotate toward your pulling side.

If you just want to correct your line of travel, you can pull or push with just one oar for a couple of strokes until the raft straightens out. Pulling back on your left oar turns the boat to the left; pulling with the right moves you right. Pushing with your left oar turns the raft right; pushing with the right will cause you to head left.

Pushing with one oar and pulling with the other will spin your raft around when you want to change direction.

Practice turning your raft using different combinations of strokes. When you are just starting out it can be hard to remember which way the boat will move in response to a pull or push on one side or the other. One trick is to remember that your pulling stroke is the strongest stroke and will always turn the raft in that direction.

Shipping your oars

In tight spots on the river, you may need to ship your oars to pass through obstacles without damaging the oars. One technique is to push your hands all the way forward to bring your oars parallel to the side of the raft. The alternative is to pull the oars back behind you so blades come forward and parallel to the raft. Pulling your oar handles back is a bit more awkward than pushing them forward. Whatever your technique, you may need to ship your oars in a hurry. Practice this skill before you need it for real: It could prevent a broken oar, a broken rib, or a flip.

When you need to get your oars out of the way of a rock or obstacle, ship them by either pushing your hands back behind you, as this rower demonstrates, or by pushing them forward until the blades are parallel to the raft tubes.

Ferrying

As mentioned earlier, ferrying is a way to move your raft across the river without being carried downstream. Most rowers use an upstream or back ferry when they want to cross the river. The advantage to an upstream ferry is that you are facing downstream so you can see approaching hazards. You also slow the raft, giving you time to come up with a plan, pick your line, or maneuver away from an obstacle. Plus, you are using your strongest stroke—the pull stroke—so you have more power to make a move. But you lose all momentum with an upstream ferry, which, in big water where you need power, can be a problem.

Most rowers don't use front ferries—where the rower faces upstream and pushes—very often.

You'll also hear people talk about downstream ferries, by which they mean facing downstream, angling the raft, and pushing with the current to move the raft across the river. Technically this isn't a ferry, as ferries are done against the current, but the so-called downstream ferry is a useful technique for moving your raft from one part of the river to another.

The correct ferry angle depends on the strength of the river's current. If you find you are being carried downstream, you probably have too much angle. Ease off on the angle until you stop losing ground. If you are stalled out or moving upstream, let your stern swing out toward the far shore so you have more angle. It also helps to have weight forward in the raft when ferrying.

PRACTICE

Paddling and rowing come pretty naturally to most of us, particularly those who are athletes. Still, the moves are often unfamiliar, so it's worth practicing on flat water or in easy Class II rapids before you tackle something more challenging. Good technique allows you to be more effective, powerful, and in control; it also helps prevent injury.

READING WATER

While there are some nimble rafts that can dart across the water, in general, the rafts used on multiday trips perform more like buses than sports cars. And, like a bus, a raft needs time to maneuver. Your best friend in that maneuvering is going to be the power of the current. If you put your raft on the right flow, you often can avoid having to fight the force of the river to navigate your way through a rapid. Watch a seasoned Grand Canyon river guide if you get a chance. These folks know exactly where to put their rafts when they enter a given rapid. They can navigate even the most infamous rapids—Lava, Granite, Crystal—with only a few well-timed strokes. That's what we're striving for: precision and accuracy over brute strength. But to reach that goal, you have to be able to read water.

Knowing how to read water allows you to use the current to move through rapids safely.

MOVING WATER

All water flows downhill, seeking the most direct and cleanest route in its path to the sea. That flow is known as current.

The current's speed or velocity is determined by a river's volume, width, and gradient, or the steepness of the riverbed. River volume is measured according to cubic feet per second (cfs), which refers to how many cubic feet of water move past a given point in a second.

Narrow river corridors constrict water, forcing it to pile up into waves and flow faster. As the river's currents converge in tight canyons you often find turbulence. Wider rivers typically have calmer, slower water.

Rapids generally occur when the river gradient steepens, the current accelerates, the channel narrows, or the river bottom is rough. Flat pools have less gradient and deeper, slower-moving water.

Water moves slower along the riverbed than on the surface because of friction. This differentiation is known as laminar flow. You also have friction along

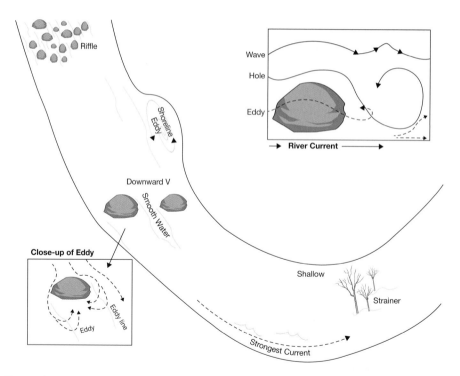

Turns, obstructions, rocks, constrictions, and gradient all affect the character of a river.
AVERY ABSOLON

RIVER LEFT AND RIVER RIGHT

When boaters talk about the different sides of a river, they use the terms "river right" or "river left," with right and left referring to your perspective as you head downstream. Whenever you hear river left, it always means your left as you face downriver. River right is always to your right while facing downstream.

the sides of the river, where the difference in the current's speed creates helical flow, or spiraling swirls of slower-moving water. This water gets pulled into the faster water in the middle of the river, and then twists down toward the bottom before being drawn back to the shore. You can see this effect when you drop a twig into the river close to shore and watch as it gets pulled out into the main current and sucked under.

All water flows downhill, but its speed and turbulence vary. Rocks, tributaries, river bends, gradient, and the tightness of the channel determine where you'll find rapids.

Eddies

Eddies are formed on the downstream side of an obstruction in the river. The obstruction slows and twists the water, causing it to turn and flow upstream behind the obstacle.

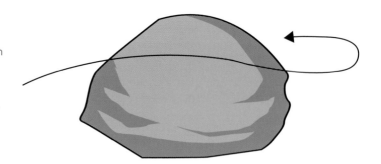

When a river's current encounters an obstruction, the water flows around that feature and then turns to fill in the void behind it, creating an eddy in which the current flows upstream.
AVERY ABSOLON

You'll find eddies along the sides of the river, on the insides of bends, and downstream of rocks or other obstacles. The water in an eddy can be calm, or, in big water, it can be swirling and violent. Rafters use eddies as a place to pull out of the main current of the river to scout, exit the boat, rest, or regroup. Being able to exit and enter eddies with confidence and ease is critical to your boating skills.

Eddies form behind obstacles that divert the flow of the current, forcing it to turn upstream. In this photo you can see eddies formed below places where the rock wall protrudes into the main flow of the river.

River bends

When the river bends, the main current is forced to the outside of the bend. Here the water will be deeper and faster than on the inside of the turn. Water piles up on the outside of the bend, cutting into the riverbank and depositing debris. Strainers or fallen trees are often found on the outside of bends.

Water on the inside of a bend moves slower and is shallower than on the outside. Sometimes that water will be too shallow to cross. You can recognize shallow water by exposed gravel, rocks, and riffles, or wavy, disturbed water.

Channels

Channels are formed when water collides with an obstruction, such as a boulder, and is forced to move around it into a channel to make its way downhill. In deeper water, these channels form an upstream V, or a tongue of smooth water that starts wide and narrows as it moves downstream. River runners look for these Vs as a safe path through shallow water or past rocks.

Rocks

A rock that projects above the surface of the water forces the current to flow around it, creating an eddy downstream.

When water flows over a rock that lies just beneath the surface, it forms a "pillow" of smooth, glassy water. You may also see an upside-down V downstream of a rock. Unlike an upstream V that indicates a channel, the upside-down or downstream V indicates a submerged obstacle that is diverting the flow of the current. Watch out for these Vs as the obstacle may not be submerged enough to allow a raft to pass over without getting snagged. In general, it's best to avoid them.

Water also pillows up against rocks that break the river surface. These pillows are frothy and turbulent. They show that the water has hit a solid obstacle and is piling up and collapsing down around the edges as it continues downstream.

Undercut rocks will not have a big pillow because much of the water flows down under the obstacle rather than around it. Undercut rocks are extremely dangerous for swimmers or small crafts because they can get trapped beneath them. Too many fatalities have taken place under such rocks, so it's important to recognize and avoid them. On popular rivers, undercut rocks are often known and identified hazards, which helps you avoid them.

Water has piled up on the rock in the center of this photograph, forming a smooth pillow upstream and a frothy hole downstream.

Waves

Water speeds up as it flows over submerged boulders or is constricted in a narrowing channel, and then stacks up downstream into standing waves. As you increase a river's volume and velocity, these waves get bigger and can form a line called a wave train. Waves remain stationary in the river, although the water molecules themselves continue moving downstream. Rafting through a bouncy wave train can be like an exciting roller-coaster ride. Make sure you know the waves are not hiding any rocks or holes that could cause you problems.

Irregularities along the riverbed such as submerged rocks as in this diagram, or constrictions in the river's channel, force water up, creating waves downstream.
AVERY ABSOLON

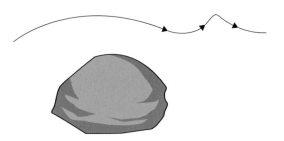

A kayaker punches through a breaking wave between two holes. Water is obviously flowing upstream in the holes while the current continues to flow downstream below the wave.

Novices often have a hard time differentiating waves from holes or frothy water piling up against a rock. Waves are usually symmetrical and have a front and backside. But not all waves are that obvious. Waves can fold back on themselves and break, creating a frothy pile that looks a lot like a rock or hole. You can distinguish rocks from breaking waves by the shape and character of the wave, but it takes practice. One easy rule is that waves will be followed by other waves, whereas a hole will have flat water behind it. Irregular waves or waves that look lower and whiter on the downstream side are generally hiding rocks. The rock may be obvious if you scout the rapid from shore, where you can view the obstacles from different perspectives.

Ultimately, if you aren't sure if something is a wave, hole, or rock, it's best to avoid it.

Rock gardens

Sections of river with lots of boulders scattered throughout are called rock gardens. Often rock gardens become most apparent at low water, when the normal channels get pinched off as the water levels drop. It can be hard to find a clean line through a rock garden.

Rock gardens are formed where landslides or tributaries scatter boulders into the river.

Holes

Holes are made when water flows over an obstacle, creating a depression below.

The obstacles are usually at or near the river surface, and often you cannot see them. Instead you see the frothing white foam of turbulent water. The river naturally refills the depression created by the obstacle by folding in on itself and moving back upstream in a recirculating flow, much like an eddy.

If enough water is recirculating, a hole can become a keeper hole that traps and holds solid objects like boats in place. Holes can be fun to go through, or they can be violent and rough and can cause you to capsize.

Boaters say that smiling holes, or hole where the sides point downstream, are safer because they have definite exit points at the sides, where the water is mov-

When obstacles, such as rocks or boulders, are at or near the surface of the river, water drops down over the obstacle creating a depression below it. The current then twists back in on itself to refill the depression, resulting in a frothy, turbulent hole.
AVERY ABSOLON

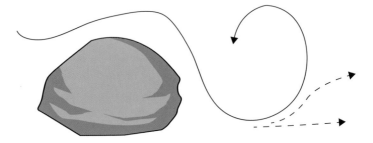

This cataraft is entering a classic hole, which is created by water flowing down over a submerged obstacle to create a depression that the river fills by turning upstream and flowing into the void.

ing out and downriver, so you get flushed downstream if you come out of your boat. Frowning holes, where the sides point upstream or frown, tend to be more difficult to get out of, especially for a swimmer or a light raft. As you travel to the edge of a frowning keeper hole, you may find yourself surfed back into the middle. Frowning holes are best to avoid, especially when you are first learning.

It can be hard to see if a hole is smiling and frowning, especially as the whitewater gets more turbulent, so if in doubt, avoid big holes. If you do get caught in a keeper hole, often the only way out is to come out of your boat and dive down under the water so you can swim below the churning currents that are holding you in place. If you cannot determine whether a hole is dangerous, try to avoid it.

Low-head dams

Low-head dams run across a river channel creating a barrier. At certain water levels the current flows over such dams, making them look safe to drop. Low-head dams are hazardous, however. A dam doesn't have to be high to cause problems. Water going over the dam creates a recirculating hole at its base. But

Low-head dams can create a recirculating hole that is a dangerous barrier for boaters.

unlike a hole formed by a boulder, there is no side to the hole below a dam. Boaters can get caught in the back current, flipped, and trapped. Many boaters have drowned in the turbulence below a low-head dam. Often the dams are not marked, so it behooves you to talk to people about the rivers you plan to run, and to scout ahead when your vision is obstructed.

TRIFOCAL VISION

It's fine to have a theoretical understanding of the way water moves, and even better to be able to recognize different river features, but the real trick to effective raft captaining is being able to see and respond to obstacles as you move downstream. Guides talk about having "trifocal vision," meaning they shift their focus constantly between three points. Point one is right in front of the raft, point two is 20-50 feet downstream, and point three is as far ahead as they can see.

Your near focus is to help avoid things right in front of you, some of which you cannot see until you are on top of them. Looking farther downstream allows you to see channels and obstacles, and gives you time to position your raft. Looking even farther out gives you a heads-up on what's coming your way. Shifting back and forth between these three points helps keep you from being taken by surprise by an unexpected hazard.

Rafters should constantly shift their focus from up close to farther downstream and in between to anticipate and avoid hazards.

Focus positive

The other important thing to remember when running rapids is to focus positive, or to focus on where you want to be and not what you want to avoid. If you are a skier or a biker, you know that you tend to drift toward objects if you stare at them. The same is true on the river. Focus your gaze on the channel or current you are heading for and not at the rock that you are trying to miss.

Humans tend to follow their eyes, which means you shouldn't look at the object you want to avoid, such as the large rock to the rafter's left.

Bumping into obstacles

Inevitably you will run into rocks and other obstacles on your way downstream. The beauty of a raft is that it tends to bounce off most of these things, especially if you hit them head-on with your bow or stern. Many beginner boaters have pinballed down rapids during their early endeavors. That's usually fine. It takes time to be able to see all the rocks ahead of you, especially in shallow rivers.

But colliding with a rock can cause you to pin or tip your raft, so it's important to know what to do when you hit one. For some reason, our natural reaction is to lean away from an obstacle we are about to collide with. Unfortunately that is the wrong reaction. Leaning away drops your upstream tube and allows water to flow over it, forcing it down and lifting the downstream tube up and onto the obstacle. You could end up stuck on the obstacle, or upside down in the river if your raft flips.

Instead, lean into the rock—a movement known as **high siding**. This keeps your upstream tube up and out of the current, and allows your raft to simply bump into and slide off the obstacle, sending you on downstream unscathed. When you are rowing, it can be hard to high side effectively from your seat, but if you have passengers and you anticipate colliding with a rock, tell them to high side or move to the side of the raft that is about to hit. In a paddle raft, the captain shouts out the high side command and all paddlers move to the rock side of the raft. Often this weight shift is enough to prevent a pin.

Leaning into, or high siding, a rock may help keep you from pinning your raft. In this photo it may be too late, as the raft's upstream tube is already underwater. High siding can keep that tube up and help you to slide off the obstacle.

In low water or on rocky rivers, rafters often soften their tubes. Soft tubes help rafts slide off rather than stick to rocks.

Finally, boaters have a couple of sayings to remind them what to do if they find themselves heading toward an obstacle they hoped to avoid. The sayings—"If you screw up, square up" and "If in doubt, straighten out"—remind you to spin your boat to hit an obstacle with your bow or stern rather than the side of your raft. Hitting an obstacle sideways makes you more likely to flip or pin.

Strainers

Strainers pose a significant hazards to all boaters, especially on smaller rivers where there isn't a lot of room to maneuver. A strainer can be created by any number of things: a fallen tree; a logjam; stray branches; a dock; anything that lets water, but not objects like paddlers or boats, flow through. A boater caught against a strainer is like a fish caught in a net or pasta left in a colander. Anything bigger than the holes will be held in place and pulled under by the relentless force of the current rushing downstream.

Strainers are created when high water from floods or spring runoff eats away at riverbanks, undercutting them until they collapse, bringing trees down that

Fallen trees in the river, known as strainers, can be dangerous hazards for boaters.

then get stuck along the riverbed. Sometimes the tree's roots remain connected to the bank, and the resulting strainer is called a sweeper. Strainer or sweeper, these hazards can be deadly.

You should always be on the lookout for strainers, especially when you are on an unknown wilderness river, on any river during spring runoff, or after a big rainstorm that causes the river to rise and erode its banks. The best way to tackle strainers is to avoid them. How? Don't run rivers in flood stage. Scout. And stay alert, particularly when you come upon blind corners.

If you see a strainer ahead, move away. Sometimes, such as in the case of a river-wide logjam, you'll be forced to portage or walk around the strainer. Other times you can ferry across the river to an open channel. Don't try to squeeze through a space in the strainer.

What do you do if you find, despite all your effort, that you are being swept into a strainer? Your best bet is to lean downstream and grab it. Forget about your raft. Haul yourself up on top the strainer. If you can, get out of the water onto the log or tree trunk. If you cannot, concentrate on keeping your head above water and scream or use your whistle to call for help.

Line dancing

When people scout a rapid or talk about the way to run one, they talk about seeing a line or path through the whitewater and out the other end. The best line is not going to be straight; rather it will be like a dance with the river as your leader. You need to follow its moves—slip down the green tongue between obstructions; use lateral waves to push one way or another; let an eddy line spin you in a new direction—basically dance your way through the obstacles using the river to lead, but making sure you follow that lead with a sense of purpose and direction. You don't want to float along like a piece of flotsam, reacting to things as you come upon them. To enable you to be proactive in the rapid, take time to scout, picking out lines with help and advice from more experienced rafters. Then hop in your raft and give it a go.

It takes a long time and a lot of experience to translate your vision of the best line into action. Subtle things can alter your dance and change things unexpectedly: you hit a rock with an oar; you have more (or less) momentum than you planned; or you didn't anticipate the way your raft would react to a hole, rock, or wave. Regardless, you won't always be able to put the dance together as well as you envisioned it onshore while scouting. That's OK. You'll get better with experience and time. You'll solidify your learning if you take a moment

Running some rapids, especially rock gardens like the one pictured here, can be like an intricate dance requiring lots of maneuvering to find the best line between obstacles.

after the run to think about how things went. Try to analyze why you ended up left when you meant to be right. Think about how your raft reacted to different obstacles. Experiment with a different plan in the next rapid. You'll figure it out.

Follow the leader

The line you run through a rapid depends on your skill level. Beginner boaters should look for the cleanest line with fewest objective hazards and the minimum number of difficult maneuvers to navigate. Advanced boaters tend to look for more challenging but still safe lines through rapids.

Often the best way for a beginner to learn to read water is to ride on a raft with an experienced rafter who points out features as you pass them by. As you gain confidence in your ability to read water and your understanding of how to maneuver your raft, you can begin to follow that person's raft in your own raft. The mother duck—or experienced boater—picks the line and demonstrates the maneuvers needed to move through the rapid efficiently. Mother-ducking works best when beginner boaters are close behind their leader. This enables them to watch their guide carefully and to mimic each and every stroke. But you'll still want to be separated by at least three or four boat lengths to give

For newer boaters it can help to follow a more experienced rafter through rapids.

yourself enough room to maneuver. If you are too close, it's easy to end up on top of each other if something goes wrong.

In mellow water, make note of what obstacles look like as you pass by so you begin to familiarize yourself with the characteristics of different features.

WHITEWATER RATINGS

The international system for river difficulty ranges from Class I to Class VI. The scale is helpful, but deceiving. Rating a river is subjective and the character of a rapid varies depending on water level and the type of boat you are using. You may also find regional variations in the way the scale is interpreted and used, meaning in some places a Class III can feel more like a Class IV, or vice versa, depending on who came up with the original rating.

Another factor to consider is whether the river is a "pool-drop" river or one continuous rapid. It's a lot easier to run a difficult rapid if you know you have a pool at the bottom, rather than miles of raging whitewater with no eddy or calm water in sight. Difficult, technical rivers pose greater threats to swimmers, as do rivers with undercut rocks or lots of downed wood creating strainers. Be conservative, especially if the water is cold or the river is remote.

INTERNATIONAL SCALE OF RIVER DIFFICULTY

Class I: Moving water with a few riffles and small waves. Few or no obstructions.

Class II: Easy rapids with small waves and clear obvious channels that do not require scouting. Some maneuvering may be required.

Class III: Rapids with high, irregular waves and narrow passages that require precise maneuvering.

Class IV: Long, difficult rapids with constricted channels that require complex maneuvering in turbulent water. The line through the rapid can be hard to determine and scouting is usually required.

Class V: Extremely long, technical, and violent rapids with tight channels that need to be scouted from shore. Rafters need to be able to make many precise, intricate moves in turbulent water to negotiate Class V rapids successfully. Rescue conditions are difficult and there is significant hazard to life in the event of a mishap.

Class VI: Class V rapids on steroids. Class VI water is nearly impossible, dangerous, and potentially life-threatening if something goes wrong. Historically Class VI rapids were downgraded to Class V once they'd been run more than a few times. Now there are Class VI rapids that are boated, but they are for experts only.

The Grand Canyon has its own 1–10 rating system, with the hardest rapids on the river getting a 10 and all others gauged in relation to those rapids.

SCOUTING RAPIDS

The best way to learn to read water and run rapids is to scout them. Scouting is also critical in difficult water or whenever you come to a horizon line, which occurs when the river drops significantly, blocking your view of what's below, or at a blind curve, where you don't know or can't see what is downstream. Scouting helps keep you out of trouble and allows you to learn to identify safe lines through turbulent water. Sometimes you can river scout by slowing your raft, standing up, and looking ahead. But if the rapid is difficult or requires a specific line, it's best to get out of your raft to take a look.

Some river guidebooks indicate whether you should scout a rapid on one side of the river or the other. Often, however, you won't have that information. Simply pull off the river in an eddy upstream of the rapid in question. Make sure the eddy is easy to get in and out of. You don't want to find yourself in trouble in the eddy with a raging rapid just below you. If in doubt, pull out higher upriver

Talking through options with other rafters while you scout rapids can help you identify the best line and improve your ability to read water.
DOT NEWTON

to scout, rather than wait until you are just above a rapid. You may have to walk a bit farther to check things out, but you won't run the risk of missing your eddy turn and getting carried into the rapid unprepared.

Don't forget to tie your raft up. It would be a bummer to have your raft float away while you are gone.

It's a good idea to carry a throw rope when you scout. That way, if someone slips and falls into the river you can help them get out. Also, you may decide to place spotters along the riverbank to watch while your party negotiates the rapid. These spotters should be armed with a throw rope to assist anyone who gets in trouble.

Wear your PFD and helmet to protect you in case you fall into the river, and so you won't forget to put those things back on when you jump into your boat to make your run.

Make sure to look at the river from different perspectives as your angle changes how things look dramatically.

Rapids change dramatically depending on your perspective. From above you can see things that you cannot see from your raft, but you also get a skewed picture of what the rapid will be like when you are on the water. Rapids usually look a lot smaller standing on shore than they do when you are in the thick of the turbulence. Obstacles like rocks and holes that are easily seen from up high may be invisible at water level. That means you need to scout from above to get an overall picture of the rapid, and then get down low so you can tell what it will look like when you are in your boat.

Find a high point that gives you a good view of the entire rapid. Look carefully at the entrance. Walk down to the end of the rapid to look at where you'll exit the whitewater. Pick out the best way to navigate through the obstacles.

As you identify your line, look for unique features that will help orient you when you are running the rapid. Such landmarks include things like distinctive boulders, overhanging trees, a prominent green tongue of water, or a bend in the river. These landmarks help you recognize places in the rapid where you need to make a move or be in a particular place, hazards you have to avoid, and where you want to be as you exit the bottom. Remember, a landmark that is clearly visible from high above the river may not be visible once you are in your raft, so make sure to pick things that you can see from the river perspective. As you walk back to your raft to make the run, stop frequently to look over your shoulder at the landmarks you've identified. They may look different from different angles, so it's a good idea to keep checking on them so you don't start down the river and realize you don't recognize anything any longer.

Visualize your route, using the landmarks you've picked out to help you remember what to do at each point. When you are first learning, it helps to go through your visualization verbally with a friend. So, for example, you'd say, "I'll enter the rapid river right close to the long black rock with my bow pointed river left. After the rock, I'll push toward the center of the river and straighten out. When I see the big square boulder midstream, I'll look for the V on its right side and push hard onto the current and into the V. Hit the wave train, pushing to maintain momentum."

While you are scouting and able to get a good look at the whole river, think about what might happen if you fail to make a critical move during your run.

Scouting helps you identify eddies like the one on the left, where you can get out of the main current to regroup, look downstream, or provide safety for other boaters.

SCOUT

Use the mnemonic SCOUT to ensure you are methodical and thorough when you are scouting.

Section: How many sections are there to this rapid and where do I want to be for each section?

Current: Where is the main current going in each section? Which current do I want to be on?

Obstacles: What obstacles—trees, rocks, etc.—do I need to be aware of?

Undercuts: Are there places where I could get pinned, or rocks I could get pulled under?

Talk: About safety and how you are going to run the rapid.

You should only run rapids you know you will be safe swimming if you make a mistake, especially when you are first starting out. If you are unsure you can do a required maneuver and you don't like the looks of a swim, get someone to row your boat for you or figure out a way to line or portage the rapid.

RAFTING SIGNALS

It can be difficult to talk or yell over the noise of the river, so it's important to know and use hand or paddle signals or a whistle to communicate. Signals are fairly uniform across the country, but go over them with your team to make sure everyone is using the same ones. Signals should be repeated back through the line of rafts to make sure everyone knows what is going on.

One whistle blow and a raised hand: "Look at me!"

Raised hand or paddle: "I confirm," "Ready," "I understand," or "Run straight down the center."

Arms out or paddle held horizontally in the air: "Stop immediately," "No."

Pointing in one direction with hand or paddle: "Go this way [whatever direction indicated by the direction of the hand or paddle]." Always point positive, i.e., where people should go. Never point at a hazard.

Three whistle blasts or waving arms or paddle: "Help," or "Emergency, stop."

Circling arm or paddle and then pointing in one direction: "Eddy out" in direction indicated.

Tap top of your head: "I'm OK."

There are other signals that can be used. For example, some people like to point to their eyes and then point in some direction indicating that they want others to look that way. You can decide with your team what signals are critical, but the ones listed above are the most commonly used.

PRACTICE, PRACTICE, PRACTICE

Learning to read water and run rapids is like learning a language. It takes time to recognize different river features and to understand how those features affect your raft. It takes time to learn how to pick a good line through whitewater and to understand the consequences of a mistake. And finally it takes time to gain a healthy respect for the power of water. So practice and find someone to coach you or be your mother duck while you learn.

CHAPTER FIVE
ON THE RIVER

One of the benefits of experience or time on the river is that you become familiar with the way your raft reacts to changing circumstances. Each raft has a slightly different feel and its load will affect that feel. The heavier and bigger your raft, the slower it will respond. On the flip side, the heavier and bigger your raft, the less it will be affected by whitewater. Big rafts tend to plow through waves and holes, flattening the turbulence with their momentum and size. Smaller rafts are bouncier and your ride may feel more like a roller-coaster than a plow.

SPEED

Your raft can travel faster, slower, or at the same speed as the current. That difference in speed is what allows you to make moves and control where your raft is going, rather than letting it being carried along at the whim of the river.

MOMENTUM

Momentum can be a rafter's best friend, or his or her nemesis. Momentum allows you to power through big waves and holes, but it also makes it harder to

Rafts need momentum to blast through big waves and holes.

make last-minute corrections, especially if you have a heavy boat. That's why it's so critical that you can identify and place yourself on the current you want to be on as you move downstream.

ANGLE

Rafters rarely face straight downstream, except when they are in flat water. Usually you'll have your raft angled slightly in anticipation of the moves you'll be making. The direction of that angle depends on whether you are pushing or pulling through the rapid.

People have different rafting styles. Some prefer to push through rapids; others like to pull. Pushing requires more finesse because you can't rely on muscles alone to avoid obstacles, but it's easier to harness the power of the current when you push. Pulling is a much stronger stroke, and so often less-experienced rafters rely on it almost exclusively. But it can be overused. It's best to practice both techniques so you are more versatile.

If you plan to pull, start by identifying the current that will take you through the rapid. Remember you'll undoubtedly need to move from one current to another as you move downstream.

Angle your boat so your bow is pointing toward any obstacle. Identify the current that will take you away from the obstacle and pull or ferry the raft onto that current and away the obstacle. Remember to allow yourself room. It can take longer than you think to make an adjustment to your direction of travel.

Rafters usually angle their rafts one way or the other in anticipation of the moves they will make downstream. This rafter is setting himself up to pull away from the hole on the left side of the bottom of the rapid.

If you are pushing, angle your bow away from any obstacles. Again, keep an eye on the currents rather than the obstacle. Your goal is not to avoid the obstacle so much as to put your raft on the flow of the river that will move you past it.

PLAN AHEAD

I've been in boats of all sizes, from a 32-foot motorized raft to a 6-foot packraft. I've canoed, kayaked (a very few times!), and duckied my way through rapids. The difference in the feel between these boats is remarkable. Kayaks are like dragonflies darting back and forth through rapids, while a tandem canoe can feel like a Ferrari when your team is in sync. Rafts are slower and more stable than these smaller boats, which means you have to plan ahead. You are not going to eddy out at the last minute to take stock of what's happening downstream unless you are lucky. You need to plan to grab that eddy well before it comes time to make the move. You also need to pick eddies that are big enough to hold your raft.

The best rafters move almost slower than the current through rapids, strategically maneuvering the raft with a few well-timed and placed strokes. Remember, like a cargo ship that takes a mile to stop, a loaded raft needs time to respond to your efforts. Look downstream, plan your moves, and don't wait until the last minute.

STABILITY

Rafts are remarkably stable crafts, but in big whitewater you can definitely flip.

To help avoid getting into a precarious position, it helps to have your paddle or oars in the water where they serve as a kind of outrigger and give you more balance. Sometimes you may just sit with your oars planted, acting as a brake or brace as you move through turbulence. Other times rowing or paddling hard allows you to break through holes and breaking waves. Rafts flip when they end up where you don't want them to be, so maintaining control of your boat and positioning it where you want to be on the current can help you avoid a spill. That said, if you are pushing your rafting skills, it's likely that at some time you will flip. We'll talk about what to do if, and when, that happens later in this guide.

USING EDDIES

As mentioned earlier, eddies make good stopping points for rafters to regroup, reconnoiter, or get off the water. Entering and exiting an eddy can be tricky in

Eddies can be helpful for slowing down, stopping to wait for the rest of your group, or staging safety. In this photo the rafter is pulling into an eddy to wait for the duckies upstream.

big rivers, where the difference in flow between the main current and the eddy acts as a barrier. That barrier is called an eddy line or eddy fence.

Eddy lines can be turbulent and powerful, and require power to punch through. Smaller eddy lines take less aggression to breach, but the principles for crossing them are the same.

Rafts need relatively big eddies to stop in. Unlike a smaller craft that can dart behind a rock for a break, with rafts you need an eddy that is about two or three times as big as your boat for it to be a good place to park. That's pretty big if you are in a 16-foot raft. For this reasons rafters rarely eddy out in the middle of rapids.

Exiting an eddy

Unlike smaller craft that tend to exit out the top of an eddy, where the eddy line is more distinct, performing what's known as a "peel out," rafters often just drift out the bottom where the eddy line is broad and ill-defined. Eddy lines spread out as you move away from the obstacle that created them, resulting in a wider area of swirly water. This water can be unstable for a small boat, but rafts are generally unaffected, so slipping out the bottom is common.

That said, it's good to practice peeling out of an eddy in your raft, because there are places where you will have no choice but to exit out the top of the eddy. To peel out, row or paddle your raft up to the top of the eddy, trying to gather some speed. Angle your boat at approximately 45 degrees to the eddy line and punch through with as much power as you can muster. Once the middle of your raft passes the eddy line, the bow paddler on the upstream side of the raft paddles forward, while the bow downstream paddler performs a draw stroke. The current will help spin the raft so it is heading downstream. With oars, the principle is the same: Once the middle of the boat passes the eddy line, the rower plants the downstream oar in the water to pivot the boat until it faces downstream.

Entering an eddy (eddy turns)

Entering an eddy is different. You usually can't sneak in at the bottom because the river's current is already pulling you downstream. Like all boaters, rafters need to aim for the top of the eddy if they want to catch it.

To catch an eddy, angle your boat roughly 45 degrees to the eddy line. The power of the river will determine whether you are best served pushing or pulling into the eddy. The more powerful the river, the more likely you will want to pull—or in a paddle raft, forward paddle—into the eddy to ensure you have enough momentum to punch through the eddy line.

In a paddle raft on a really big river, paddlers should lean into the turn to help lift the upstream tube. Remember, the direction of the current changes when you enter the eddy, so your upstream tube will actually be on the down-river side of your raft, since water flows the opposite way in an eddy. Think of banking turns on a motorcycle, and you'll get the idea of which way to lean into eddy turns. As your bow crosses the eddy line, the paddlers on the downriver side will paddle forward hard, while those on the upstream side can pause and then reach forward into the current in the eddy to spin the raft in.

In an oar rig, entering an eddy is more like a ferry. Set your angle at around 45 degrees to the eddy line and pull your raft in.

Leaving an eddy to ferry

Often your goal in leaving an eddy may be to get to the other side of the river. In this case, you may not want to do an eddy turn that will take you downstream right away, but instead want to set yourself up for a ferry. To do this, move up to the top of the eddy line at about a 45-degree angle with as much speed as possible. As you cross the eddy line, pull on the downriver side of your raft to maintain your angle and keep the current from spinning your raft. Once across the eddy line set your ferry angle to take you across the river.

DEALING WITH THE UNEXPECTED

Ideally you will always have clean runs through rapids, but we all know that's improbable when you are learning. Even when you have lots of miles under your belt things happen, so it's helpful to be aware of likely problems, and know how to respond.

We've already talked about bumping into rocks and the risk of pinning your raft. Remember to practice high siding so that your paddle crew or passengers perform the move instinctively when they anticipate a collision.

For rowers, another common problem is having your oar wrenched out of your hand when you hit a rock, which can hurt you and/or break your oar. If you see a rock coming your way and have time, ship your oars to avoid contact with the obstacle. Focus on your downstream oar, as that is the one that will get you into trouble if it comes in contact with a rock or the river bottom. Sometimes, however, you can't see obstacles underwater or don't have time to react. Your best bet if your oar collides with something hard is to just let go of the oar handle to avoid dislocating your shoulder or some other injury. But beware of a loose oar flying around. That, too, is hazardous, and can cause injury.

In shallow rivers it is not uncommon for oars to pop out of the oarlock after hitting a rock. If that happens your best bet is to let go of the oar handle to avoid injury. Here a rafter comes upon a lost oar midstream.

Ejection

Getting ejected from a raft is more common than actually flipping. To help stay inside, make sure you have a secure position and your feet are braced under the thwarts, in the foot cups or against the frame. Passengers should make sure they have something secure to hang on to before the raft enters a rapid.

Actively paddling or rowing helps you stay in an athletic position and makes you better able to absorb the shock of a sudden change of direction. But if you ram a rock hard or hit some big waves unexpectedly, it's easy to get pitched out of the raft.

In big whitewater, you may have your paddlers or passengers drop down into the bottom of the raft as you approach big waves or holes. They are more stable in the bottom, and less likely to fall out of the raft.

The first thing to do if you do find yourself in the water is stay calm. Get your feet up to the surface so they aren't dangling where they could get entrapped by a rock. Keep your mouth closed, and relax.

It's easy to get tipped off balance and ejected from your raft if it hits a rock or hole with a lot of force.

If you find yourself in the water, stay calm, keep your mouth closed, and relax.

Beginner kayakers often are told to count to ten while hanging upside down before they try to roll up so they have time to compose themselves. Seconds can feel like hours when you find yourself unexpectedly in the river, especially in big whitewater. But if you panic you'll only make things worse. Close your mouth, hang on to your paddle if you have one, and take stock of your situation. What comes next depends on where you are.

Swimming

If you come up alongside the raft, try to grab on. Your teammates may be able to haul you back on board in a matter of seconds. But beware. The raft can become a hazard if you are between it and an obstacle. If you are downstream or cannot get back to the side of the boat, move away from it so you aren't in danger.

The defensive swimming position is on your back with your feet up at the surface and pointing downstream. This position allows you to fend off rocks with your feet rather than your head. In big rapids, you won't be able to do much else, as it's hard to swim with any effectiveness in the turbulence. Usually you just have to wait until you get to the bottom of the rapid before you can consider other options.

If you go for a swim and come up close to the raft, one of your teammates may be able to pull you back in right away.

The defensive swimming position is on your back, feet downstream and up, ready to kick off rocks and other obstacles. If you can, you want to keep hold of your paddle as well.

FOOT ENTRAPMENT

Do not try to stand up in moving water if it is above your knees. It's easy to get a foot stuck in between rocks along the river bottom. Falling forward with your foot trapped can be deadly. The force of the current holds you down, making it very difficult to free yourself. It's even difficult for rescuers to help someone in this situation. The best way for swimmers to avoid this danger is to wait to stand up until the water is well below their knees and the current is mild.

The aggressive swimming position is on your belly. If you want to get somewhere to avoid a hazard or move to safety, flip over onto your stomach and swim in the direction you want to move. Kick hard for power and to keep your feet up. Freestyle is your most powerful stroke, so if you need to get somewhere fast, do the front crawl. If you have more time and want to assess the situation but still move, try breaststroke.

Try to hang on to your paddle if you have one. It can be hard to swim with a paddle in your hand. The trick to keeping tabs on it when you want to swim is to toss it out in front of you 5 feet or so, chase it down, and toss it again until you get to your destination.

It can also be hard to get your breath in the midst of whitewater. Try to time it so that you breathe while down in the trough between waves. Usually waves will break in your face at the top, making it hard to get a breath up there. Try also to keep your mouth closed in between breaths to avoid taking in a mouthful by accident.

Ideally your teammates may be able to grab you from the boat or throw a rope to you to help you to shore. You may also be able to swim to an eddy or the raft when the water calms. In this case, turn on to your stomach and swim hard for your destination.

FLIPPING

If a paddle raft flips, the crew is usually flung far and wide as the boat overturns. In this case everyone should react as described above. If you end up in the water upstream of your raft, you can try to scramble on top or hold on as the raft moves downstream. This way you can help move the raft to shore after the rapid.

In big, technical rivers, it's a good idea to think about the consequences of an unintended swim while you are scouting. Your decision about what to do if you end up in the water may be determined by what lies below. If you know there is a hazard you prefer to avoid, you may want to swim hard away from it rather than float through the rapid on your back.

If you end up underneath the raft, don't panic. It can actually be rather calm under there, especially if you end up in an air pocket. Reach up until you feel the raft and then use your hands to walk yourself to an edge where you can get out from underneath. Ideally you'll find yourself upstream, but if you do end up downstream of the raft, move away as quickly as possible so you aren't in between the raft and any upcoming obstacle.

Oar rigs are less likely to flip than paddle rafts because the oars serve as out-riggers and help balance the raft. But it does happen. Flipping a raft where the cargo has not been secured properly can be dangerous, as there are lots of hard objects that can hit you and cause injury. Plus, you'll lose your gear if it's not tied down. The oars can also be an objective hazard. For this reason, make sure your cargo is lashed down securely at all times. You never know when you might flip.

Once you are in the water, your goal is to either get on top of your raft, or get away and upstream of it until you are safely through any rapids.

We'll go into up-righting an overturned raft in Chapter Thirteen: Basic River Rescue.

MOVING YOUR GROUP THROUGH RAPIDS

If you've ever been on a big commercial whitewater river run, you are probably familiar with seeing lines of rafts stretched upstream of rapids. On wilderness rivers, you may be lucky and have only your own group to contend with, or you may need to practice a little river etiquette to avoid a tangled mess when you come to rapids.

It's nice to have room to maneuver through whitewater. If you end up right on top of another raft, it can add stress and complication to your run. Give yourself at least three boat lengths, and watch the raft in front of you. If it has slowed or stopped, you may need to slow or stop to avoid closing the gap between the two boats too quickly. If a rapid is complex and requires a lot of precise, technical moves, you are probably best off running it one at a time. This allows you to have safety boats positioned in eddies, and people with throw bags standing on shore.

If you bump into another party, river etiquette is that the first party to arrive has the right-of-way. Let that group go first, unless they have elected to scout something you plan to run right through. If they are onshore, you are fine to

You provide support for the rest of your party, so when moving through rapids keep your group close enough together to help each other if something goes wrong, but with enough room between boats to maneuver.

run the rapid. If they are getting back into their boats to hit the water, it's polite to check in to see if it is OK to go ahead in front of them. Or pull over and let them go first.

Remember, you are all out there seeking the same thing, so be polite and generous with the people you meet on the river.

There is no rule for determining the proper order of boats in your own group when moving through a rapid. In general, it's nice to have a more experienced team out front and in the back, with the less experienced rafters sandwiched in between.

Unless you are on a super easy river, regroup at the bottom of rapids to ensure everyone gets through OK, or to provide help if they did not.

TIPS FOR BEING SAFE ON THE RIVER

- *Always wear your life jacket.* Most river fatalities include the absence of a PFD, the use of alcohol, flooded rivers, and/or hypothermia. A lifejacket can save your life if worn correctly. Don't underestimate how hard it can be to swim in rapids, and make sure you wear your PFD through all whitewater.
- *Wear your helmet in rapids.* Your brain is precious. You can protect it by wearing a helmet when there's even the slightest chance you may be swimming in turbulent water.
- *Wear the right clothes.* As mentioned earlier, hypothermia is often a factor in river fatalities. Make sure to wear the proper clothing for the conditions you expect to encounter on the river. Carry a dry bag with extra layers just in case.
- *Know what to do if you end up in the water.* The downriver swimmer's position is on your back, feet up and facing downstream, knees slightly bent to absorb shock if you bump into a rock. Try to keep your butt up so it doesn't drag along the bottom. Your arms should be out at your sides to help you maintain control. If you decide to actively swim to safety, turn over onto your stomach, point your body in the direction you want to go, and swim hard.
- *Know the plan.* Listen to your captain if you are part of a paddle crew. Listen to your expedition mates if you are rowing your own rig with other rafters. Make sure everyone understands the plan and knows how to communicate with hand or paddle signals.
- *Stay calm.* Panicking is a waste of time and energy. If you end up in the water, you'll want all the energy you can muster to get yourself back in the raft or out of the river, so don't use it up flailing and screaming in fear. Take a deep breath and relax.

CHAPTER SIX

PLANNING A MULTIDAY RIVER TRIP

Once you have your basic rafting skills down, it's time to go on a multiday trip. That's what river life is really all about, at least in my book.

As mentioned earlier, you can approach a river trip in different ways. There's the "everything but the kitchen sink" plan, and the go-light boating backpacker method. Your choice depends upon the size of your raft, the number in your group, the nature of the river, and your personal preference. This book will discuss both options.

PLANNING

Permits

Most popular whitewater rivers requires a permit during the high seasons. These permits are often given out through a lottery system that takes place months before the launch date. If you are interested in securing a river permit, get online as much as a year in advance of your desired trip to find out what you need to do to get a permit. Many people mark their calendars each year to remind them to put in for river permits on a certain date.

For popular rivers, such as the Middle Fork of the Salmon or the Colorado though the Grand Canyon, permits are highly coveted and the lotteries competitive. Securing a permit for such rivers is never guaranteed. It's helpful to have all your team members apply for a permit to increase your odds of success, but don't be surprised if you don't get what you want. It can take years to get a permit on some rivers.

Some outfitters offer "row your own" hybrid trips. Just what this looks like varies from outfitter to outfitter. It may be you use an outfitter's permit but

Permits for popular rivers are distributed through a competitive lottery. It can take years to get a Grand Canyon permit.
STEFANIE VANDAELE

bring all your own gear. It may be the outfitter provides the gear and a guide or two, but you and your colleagues do all the rowing. Or it may be something in between. The advantage of working through an outfitter is that often you can secure a specific date for your trip, which is helpful if you have a tight schedule. You may also find a guide willing to give you pointers on your rafting technique, plus guides usually know rivers well, so they can help you pick lines through rapids. Usually these hybrid trips are less expensive than a fully guided expedition. It's worth asking outfitters if they are willing to consider such an option, especially if you and your entire team get skunked in the lottery.

If you have a flexible schedule, you may also be able to secure a permit after someone else cancels. You can sometimes get on a list to be notified of last-minute openings for the river you desire, or you can check in periodically to see if something has opened up. Some rivers have a low season when permits are not required. All this information can be found online.

When you have secured a permit, read it carefully. River permits have very exacting requirements for how to camp and what to bring on your trip. You may have to show rangers each piece of equipment at the put-in, and often they'll ask for identification to verify the members of your team, so it's important to follow the rules.

YOUR TEAM

A successful river trip requires a fair bit of planning. First and foremost is the task of coming up with a compatible team.

You may have a group of regulars with whom you boat, but if not, it's helpful to think about the following in pulling together your team.

Pulling together your team takes some forethought. You need boaters capable of navigating the river, plus you want a group that gets along well and has similar goals.

Skills

It's fine to have a wide range of experience and skill on your team as long as you have the basic requirements for the river in question covered. You need to have boaters who are comfortable navigating any rapids you will encounter on the trip. You need people familiar with river travel, packing, camping, and rescue. If you do not know some of the people on your trip, ask them about their experience before you commit. Often it helps to have a personal recommendation from someone you trust to ensure an individual you do not know is competent and will be a good fit with your group.

You can have a wide range of boating abilities in your group as long as there are enough competent rafters to navigate any rapids you expect to encounter.

Goals

To help make your trip as smooth as possible, make sure everyone on your team has similar goals. You may be traveling with a group that has been on the river many times together, in which case you probably don't need to spend any time figuring out goals. But if it's your first time with the group, it's important to talk about what you want to happen. If half your group likes to party all night long and the other goes to bed at 8 p.m. and rises at 6 a.m., you could have a problem.

Ask your teammates what they hope to get out of the trip, how they like to live on the river, how long they want to spend on the water each day, and

PRE-TRIP PLANNING
- Permit
- Team selection
- Campsite selection (if designated on permit)
- Shuttle
- Group gear
- Emergency communications: SPOT personal locator device, inReach satellite communicator, satellite phone, or nothing
- Food and meal schedule
- Chore schedule
- Leadership
- Group goals
- Skills assessment and safety plan
- End-of-trip cleanup plan

whether they want to hike, party, or just hang out on the beach. Make sure everyone understands how chores will be accomplished, who's in charge, and what the trip will cost. You can accomplish a lot of this communication over e-mail, or have a face-to-face meeting a few months before the trip to ensure everyone is on the same page. It sucks to get out on the river and find out that the group is not getting along, that one person is doing all or none of the work, or that you can't trust someone's judgment.

Leadership
Most groups function better if they have some kind of leadership structure. With highly experienced teams that have worked together in the past, you can have a pretty casual setup, but even then it's critical that someone is making sure you have everything you need before you launch, and that the entire group knows what is going on during the trip.

Often the de facto leader is the permit holder. He or she usually invites others on the trip and organizes the logistics before you launch, but once you are on the river that person doesn't have to be in charge.

To figure out how you want to function as a team, take a few minutes to talk to your group. You may want to designate a formal leader who delegates tasks and makes sure that everything is in order. That person doesn't have to be in charge all the time, but he or she is responsible for ensuring that everyone knows the drill and is comfortable with the day's plan. On the river, leadership often goes to the most experienced team member, who keeps the group together and

River trips are fun; they also can be risky. It helps to have a designated leader to help your group find a balance between fun and safety.

makes sure everyone gets through all the rapids safely. Off the water, anyone can be in charge as long as the group knows and respects that individual.

It can be tricky to balance safety and fun on river trips. The best trip leaders are able to walk that line by demonstrating respect for their team, a willingness to listen to and incorporate the opinions of others in all decision-making, and an ability to recognize when to be serious and when to lighten up and goof around.

Group chores can be handled in any number of ways, but it's nice to have some kind of agreed-upon system so one or two people don't end up doing the lion's share of the work. Typical chores include unloading rafts; setting up the kitchen, toilet, and hand-washing stations; cooking meals; cleaning dishes; storm-proofing camp at night, and breaking down camp each day before launching on the river. Some people like to have a cook team prepare all the meals and do the dishes for a day at a time, leaving the rest of the group to do other chores or chill out. You may prefer to have separate cook and cleanup teams for each meal. You may decide to all cook together. Whatever method you opt for, make sure everyone understands what is expected to avoid tension and share the load.

Most groups function best with some kind of chore schedule so that work is shared among the team members equitably.

It's a good idea for group members to check in with each other in the morning, before you get on the water, so everyone has a chance to look at the map and knows what is going on that day. This includes sharing information about the number of miles you're traveling, the rapids you will encounter, boat order, your intended campsite, etc. This can also be a time when the group talks about any issues that have arisen, such as whether you are going through toilet paper faster than anticipated, or if something is going on among team members that needs to be discussed. This doesn't have to be a formal, rigid meeting. It's just time for a quick check-in, but if you make something like that part of your daily routine then when you do have an issue that needs addressing, you have a structure in place to allow for it.

It's nice to check in with your team—even the kids—before you hit the water so people know what the plan for the day is.

LOGISTICS

Planning your trip involves making sure you have all the equipment, food, and information you need for the river, and that you have your transportation to and from the river worked out.

Shuttle

Part of your pretrip planning includes figuring out how you will shuttle your cars to the takeout. You can run your own shuttle, but on long rivers that is usually impractical as the shuttle can involve days of driving to get all cars to the right spot. Most rivers have outfitters who will shuttle your vehicles for a fee.

Boating season gets busy, so it's important to make your reservation early. You can search the Internet for shuttle drivers by entering the name of your river and the word shuttle, and usually you will find a number of options. You can also ask around with friends who've made the trip for recommendations.

River guides and maps

If no members of your group have been on the river you plan to descend, it's important that at least someone does some research about what to expect

Most popular rivers have some kind of map and guide that tells you about what you'll find as you head downstream.

before you hit the water. Most popular rivers have some kind of river guide that describes everything from the rapids you will encounter to the campsites, hikes, history, and sometimes the flora, fauna, and geology you'll find along the way.

In addition to a river guide, you can talk to people about the trip to get more detailed information. Helpful resources include river rangers, guiding outfits, and the Internet. These resources can give you current river conditions, updates on campsites, and even the beta on things like bugs, or whether bears, skunks, or mice are hanging out in campsites.

On some rivers, you are required to choose your campsites when you purchase your permit, so it's a good idea to know how far you want to travel each day and which campsites fit that schedule before finalizing your permit. It's also a good idea to consider things like sun exposure when you select your sites. In the summer you may want to look for shade, while in the fall or spring you may want full sun, especially in the mornings when you're trying to get out of camp. River levels and group size are also factors to consider in selecting your sites.

Finally, if you want to hike or leave the river, bring a topographic map of the area and maybe a GPS to help you navigate.

RIVER GEAR

We've discussed some of the basic river gear you will need in previous chapters, but it's good to have a checklist to help make sure nothing gets left behind.

The amount of gear required for a multiday raft trip—especially a twenty-one-day Grand Canyon trip—can be staggering.
DOT NEWTON

River Gear Checklist

- Raft: The number and size of rafts you need depends on your group size and the length of the trip.
- Oars or paddles: One or two extra per raft; check permit requirements
- Oar frame
- Lash straps: Assorted lengths for lashing the frame to the raft and securing dry boxes, coolers, dry bags, and other cargo in place. Loop straps—which have a loop of webbing in each end to girth hitch to the frame—are useful for dry boxes and coolers.
- PFD: One per person, plus one extra per raft (each should be fitted with a whistle)

- Helmet: Optional, depends on the river
- First aid kit: One per boat, with an additional large kit for the group
- Raft repair kit: Details on what to include are in Chapter Fourteen: Basic Repair and Maintenance.
- Pin kit: Details on what to include are in Chapter Thirteen: Basic River Rescue.
- Dry boxes: One or two per raft
- Cooler: One per raft
- Sponge, bucket
- Throw bag
- One or two sand stakes and a mallet per group for anchoring rafts at night if you are on a river with large sandy beaches. Sand stakes aren't necessary on rivers with lots of trees and rocky campsites.

CAMPING EQUIPMENT

You don't need everyone on your trip to bring all the gear needed, so before your trip create a gear list and consult with your team members to determine who's bringing what. If you are missing a critical piece of gear you may be able to rent it from an outfitter, or if you have plenty of advance notice, someone on your team can purchase the item before the trip.

Kitchen

The bulk of your group gear is going to be kitchen gear. Here you can be either elaborate or streamlined, depending on your menu, the weather, the style of trip you plan, and its length. You'll find the standard river kitchen is pretty well stocked, almost like your kitchen at home in terms of tools and equipment. But you don't have to follow that system. If you prefer to go light, take cues from your backpacking days and pare things down to the essentials. That means nothing more than a one-burner stove, fuel, a large pot or two depending on your group size, and maybe a frying pan. You'll want a pot grips or wool gloves to handle pots, and a spatula is important if you plan to fry anything. But otherwise, like backpackers, you can sit on the ground to cook and forgo the extravagance of tables, chairs, coolers, and heavy, bulky kitchen boxes.

The classic river trip includes a well-stocked kitchen and elaborate meals.

That said, it's fun to have the ability to have nice meals on a river trip, and most boaters enjoy a cold beverage at the end of a hot day, so unless you have a reason for going super light, bring a bit more gear and set up an efficient, comfortable kitchen for your cooking needs.

Suggested Group Gear for a Fully Stocked Trip

Kitchen Gear	Primary Equipment	Extras	Details
Folding river tables	2–3 large tables for prep, cooking, and dishwashing	1 small table for drinks	Long narrow tables work well because they can be strapped on top of a dry box or across the frame in the raft and/or serve as seating for passengers.
Mesh dish hammock	1 large for dishes, pots, and pans	1 small for utensils	Dish hammocks should be able to hang from tables.

Kitchen Gear	Primary Equipment	Extras	Details
Stove	2–6 burners	Propane sufficient for entire trip	2 lighters and waterproof matches
Blaster (optional)	1 burner; 65,000 BTUs for boiling water quickly		Particularly nice for big groups in the winter, when you want hot water fast, and to expedite dishwashing.
Wash bins (plastic bins, metal pails, or collapsible buckets)	3–4 metal wash pails are nice if you want to heat dishwater in the pail.	Bleach and dish soap stored in a small mesh bag for transport	Dish towels, sponge, Brillo pad, or scrubby
Pots and pans	1 large pot for heating water; 1 large pot for meal preparation; 1 smaller pot for cooking; 1–2 large skillets and/or a griddle	1–2 Dutch ovens for baking and casseroles	2 hot pads or pot grips for moving hot pans around
Stainless steel or plastic mixing bowl	1–2, depending on the size of your group		
Coffee-making equipment	Insulated bottles and cone filters, coffee press, etc.		
Utensils	1 spatula, 1 can opener, 2 large spoons, 2 large knives, cheese grater, tongs, peeler, kitchen scissors, measuring spoons and cups, corkscrew, etc.		
Cutting boards	1–2 (plastic sheets pack well in dry boxes)		
Strainer		For removing food particles from dishwater	Usually required on most permitted rivers

Kitchen Gear	Primary Equipment	Extras	Details
Cups, mugs, bowls, plates, and silverware	1 of each for every team member		
Trash compactor bags and ziplock bags of assorted sizes			
Toilet setup	Determine capacity by the number of days and the number of people on the trip.	Toilet seat, toilet paper (some people like special toilet paper designed for RVs), toilet deodorizer, hand sanitizer, sanitizing wipes	Extra 5-gallon bucket to use as a "pee bucket" next to the groover.
Miscellaneous	Paper towels; bee or wasp traps; bug repellant; aluminum foil; a mallet to crush cans; survey tape or duct tape for marking things		
Dry boxes	1–2 per raft; cardboard boxes or milk crates that fit inside dry boxes are helpful for organizing food	1 dry box should serve as the kitchen box and contain all pots, pans, utensils, and other cooking and eating supplies	
Large (20 millimeter) ammo/rocket boxes	2–4 ammo/rocket boxes are useful for garbage, recyclables, and ash as they are emptied of food or beer. People also use grain sacks or large rice bags for trash and recyclables.		
Lantern with extra batteries	Helpful for fall or spring trips with short days		Inflatable, solar-powered LED lanterns work well.
1 scrim cloth kitchen floor	Good for keeping camp clean and collecting food scraps		Kitchen floors are required on most rivers.

Kitchen Gear	Primary Equipment	Extras	Details
Fire pan with grill and cover	Fire cloth, folding shovel, ash container (can be an ammo can)	Charcoal briquettes impregnated with lighter fluid	Fire pans are required on some rivers regardless of whether you intend to build a fire or not.
Rain or shade canopy			
Water jugs	Capacity for roughly 1 gallon per person per day. Many rivers have places where you can stock up on fresh water mid-trip, which will affect the number of jugs you need.	Water filter or purification system	
Chairs	1 per person		Consider one extra on long trips as chairs often break.
First aid and drug kit	For longer trips it's worth talking to your doctor about the pain medications and antibiotics you should carry.	See the Appendix for a checklist.	
Maps, river guide	It's nice to have a river map for each raft.		
Communications device	Depending on the remoteness of your trip, you may want to include a SAT phone or personal locating beacon in case of an emergency. You cannot get cell phone coverage in many river corridors because of the canyon walls.		

Suggested Group Gear for Going Light (group size 4–6)

Kitchen	Main gear	Extras
	1–2 single-burner backpacking stoves, cartridge mixed-fuel stoves, or white gas stoves. You can also cook on fires in some places.	Fuel, lighter, waterproof matches
	1 pot per stove	Wool gloves or pot grips
	1 cup, bowl, spoon per person (can use cup as bowl and leave bowl behind)	
	Dry box or dry bag for group gear and food	Trash compacter bags and grain or rice sack for garbage
	Portable light (inflatable LED, solar-powered lantern)	
Water bag or jugs	1 5-gallon jug to carry drinking water	1 water bag to hang up for handwashing
Toilet setup	River toilet or personal system for packing out waste, such as WAG bags	Toilet paper, hand soap, hand sanitizer
Communication device	SAT phone or personal locating beacon	
First aid and drug kit		
Maps		

Note: On most permitted rivers you are required to carry certain equipment, such as fire pans and kitchen floor cloths. If you want to go light, talk to the land management agency in charge of the river to find out if it allows substitutions to cut weight, such as using an aluminum roasting pan for a fire pan, or bags designed for transporting human waste, such as WAG bags.

Kitchen setup

You'll find a variety of opinions on the best way to set up a river kitchen. All are fine. Your goal is to have your kitchen be as convenient and efficient as possible, just like at home. A good standard setup is to set up two long river tables in an L-shape, with the dish rack hammock suspended from one table and your stove set up on the other. With big groups, you may want to have three tables arranged in a U-shape, as well as a fourth, small table for drinks. Lay your kitchen floor out between the tables so you can cook and prep

You'll find all sorts of ways to set up your kitchen, but the classic is a U-shaped kitchen with a couple of prep tables and a table for dishwashing. This group opted to bring their coolers and dry boxes up to camp. You can also leave them on the boat and just bring up what you need at mealtime.

without worrying about food scraps. Anything you drop will be caught on the floor so you can clean it up easily later.

Most people like to bring their kitchen box, with all the utensils, pots, pans, and dishes, up to the kitchen at every camp. This just makes life easier, as you don't have to run down to the raft every time you need a spoon or knife. Food, on the other hand, often stays on the boats. The simplest technique is to take a shopping bag down to the rafts before each meal to get all the items you need for that meal.

Food organization in the raft is critical, especially for longer trips. Many people put cardboard boxes or milk crates inside their dry boxes to create bins that allow them to organize their stuff. Wine boxes with internal dividers can work well. On longer trips, such as the Grand Canyon, you can use rocket boxes or large ammo cans to hold each day's food. These boxes can be used as trash containers after they are emptied. Coolers may be divided by meals or by contents; for example, you can have meat, produce, and dairy coolers, with those holding food for later in the trip taped shut to help them stay cold.

Depending on the length of the trip, you can arrange your food in different ways. The simplest technique is to have everything separated out by meal, but on longer trips you may not have the space to do that. One efficient system is to put four boxes in your dry box, one for breakfasts, one for lunches, and one for dinners, with the fourth for drinks and snacks. You can also opt to have staples, such as pasta and rice, in one place, crackers and bread in another, canned goods, etc., in yet another, and so on. The key is to have a system that everyone understands so your supplies don't get mixed up and confused every time someone digs in to search of a specific item.

See Chapter Eight: Food for more details on menu planning and cooking organization.

River stoves

Most likely you will use either a two- or four-burner—maybe even a six-burner—propane stove on your river trip. You can use any model stove for this purpose, but it's worth looking at Partner Steel's aluminum stoves, which are

You can use a classic Coleman two-burner stove or a more specialized Partner Steel four-burner for your river trip.

HOW MUCH PROPANE?

The amount of fuel you need on a river trip depends on the number of people in your group, the type and style stove you are using, the length of the trip, and the expected weather conditions. In addition, if you have any other fuel demands—a blaster or lantern for example—you'll need additional fuel.

In general, you can expect to use one 5-gallon (20 pound) propane tank every eight days on a summer trip with a group of sixteen people. Most Grand Canyon trippers bring at least three tanks on a twenty-one-day trip to be on the safe side. For a five-day Main Salmon trip, you'll probably only need one tank—unless you are bringing a blaster, in which case you'll need a second tank; however, you can bring a smaller size for the blaster.

Round those numbers up for a winter trip and down if you have fewer people.

made with river-running in mind. Some of Partner Steel's models are built to fit inside ammo cans and dry boxes. The two-burner version folds in half for easy storage, and the 18-inch model is designed so you can have two 9-inch frying pans side-by-side while cooking. Partner Steel also makes a stove stand for some of its stoves. Partner Steel's products are tough, durable, and reliable.

One of these 5-gallon tanks of propane should last a group of sixteen about eight days on a summer trip.

For big groups it's nice to have a "blaster," or a 65,000 BTU burner that boils water quickly.
STEFANIE VANDAELE

Handwashing stations

It's nice to have at least one handwashing station in camp for food preparers and for people to use after they go to the bathroom. The simplest handwashing system is a water bag hanging from a tree with soap nearby, but on most river trips people use 5-gallon buckets and a foot pump with a spout that fits on the edge of the bucket to create a hands-free handwashing station. If you really want convenience, make a holder for your soap dispenser that can hang off the bucket and keep the soap out of the sand.

You can find handwashing setups online—NRS and Partner Steel each make one—or if you are handy, you can create your own.

River water is fine to use for handwashing, but if you plan to use that water for other purposes—say to rinse out a coffee press—add half a capful of bleach just to be on the safe side.

You can help prevent the spread of illness by making sure everyone has clean hands. Easy-to-use, convenient hand-washing stations like this one make good hygiene easy.
STEFANIE VANDAELE

RIVER TOILETS

Known as the groover, the unit, or the loo with a view, river toilets are something everyone must use at some point on their float. Back in the old days, people used to poop in 20-millimeter (mm) rocket boxes without a seat. This left indents in their butts, which resulted in the nickname "groover" for the river toilet. That practice is long gone. Even those who continue to use rocket boxes now carry toilet seats that fit on top for comfort. But the name has stuck, and many boaters still call their river toilet the groover.

The best groover on the market, in my book, is manufactured by Partner Steel and is called the Jonny Partner. There are other options: ECO-Safe Toilet System, Selway Fabrications, and Coyote Portable Toilet System all make good river toilets, or you can just use a rocket box with a toilet seat. For short trips people sometimes use WAG bags or other disposable systems for packing out poop, although not all river regulations allow this kind of waste management technique. Check before you head to the put-in to make sure your system is approved. If you plan

A Jonny Partner portable toilet sits in a scenic spot ready for use.

to do a lot of river trips I highly recommend the Jonny Partner, although on long Grand Canyon trips rocket boxes pack a bit more easily.

Groovers come with an estimated capacity, enabling you to figure out how many you need for your river trip. The Jonny Partner is estimated to hold roughly 50-60 uses, so if you have a party of ten, one Jonny Partner should last you for approximately five days. Different models have different capacities, so make sure you check if you are going with another brand. On long trips it's a good idea to be generous in your figuring. No one wants to run out of groover space.

To save space and control odors, don't pee in the groover. Most river guidelines require people to pee in the river. You can place your groover on the shore close to the river so people can pee before they poop, or (and I personally prefer this method) bring a 5-gallon bucket for peeing. You can empty the pee bucket into the river at the end of your stay in camp.

For groups of sixteen or less you can usually get by with one to two rolls of toilet paper per day. Encourage people to go easy on the TP. That helps conserve groover space and keeps your needs down. TP goes into the groover. If you are on a long trip, extra TP rolls can be stored in the empty groovers until needed. Otherwise, bring a 20 mm rocket box or spare dry bag to hold the toilet seat, TP, hand sanitizer, bleach wipes (for wiping down toilet seat) and a dry bleach or chemical deodorizer, such as Campa-Chem RV-holding tank deodorizer. Campa-Chem is sold at Walmart and RV camping supply stores. If you go the deodorizer route, start with one packet in an empty groover and add another when it's half full. You can also use a product known as Groover Tamer to help with odors. Groover Tamer is expensive ($70 for one packet designed for an eighteen-day trip) but the product is supposed to be environmentally safe and many people swear by it.

Groover setup is a critical daily chore. It's one of the first things to be established when you make camp. If you are on groover duty, look for a private spot away from camp, near the river, and with a good view. Place the groover on level ground, remove the lid, and put the toilet seat in place. If you have a pee bucket, set that up next to the groover. Place the TP in a handy spot inside a plastic bag and weighted down with a rock. If it's raining, you may want to store your TP in the ammo can that held your toilet seat. I like to store my toilet seat in a stuff

Setting up and taking down the portable toilet are critical daily chores. Usually it takes two people to carry a loaded groover.

sack during transit to keep it separate from the other items stored in the ammo can, such as TP and hand sanitizer.

Store all supplies—wipes, stuff sacks, deodorizer—in a closed rocket box next to the groover while in camp. Make sure the toilet seat lid is closed when the groover is not in use. That will help keep the smell down and animals out.

At the head of the trail to the groover site, place some kind of sign that indicates the groover is in use. Anything works—a bandana, a pink flamingo—use your imagination! Whoever is in the groover takes the sign along while they do their business and returns it to the head of the trail when they are done, so people know the groover is free.

Place the hand-washing station near the groover trail so people can't forget to wash up after they are done.

Typically, the groover is one of the last things to get loaded onto the boats. Whoever is on groover duty should give a last call, so people know it's time to do their business. Then, once everyone is finished, wipe the toilet seat down with a sanitizing wipe, then return it to the stuff sack and put the seat into the ammo box. Pour the pee into the river, seal up the groover, and load it onto the raft.

When your groover is full and it's time to move to a new one, leave the full groover sealed up on the boat.

Most groups like to store their river toilets on one raft.

At the end of the trip, the groover needs to be taken to an RV dump station or a SCAT machine (often found at popular river takeouts) to be emptied and cleaned. To facilitate cleaning, you can spray the insides of your groovers with PAM cooking spray or the like before the trip. That helps things slide out when you're all done.

You may want to add a little water to the groover at the start of the last day if a SCAT machine is at the takeout. If the SCAT machine is down the road, add water before you put the groover on the boat trailer. That little bit of extra fluid and some agitation from driving or rafting helps moisten the load and makes the groover easier to clean. But adding water earlier in the trip weighs down your raft and makes it cumbersome.

You may find you don't want to venture down to the shoreline in the middle of the night if you must pee. If that's the case, bring a pee bottle or bucket to your sleeping spot. You can use that during the night and empty it into the river the following morning.

TRASH

Twenty-millimeter ammo cans or rocket boxes do a little bit of everything on river trips, and holding garbage is one of their great attributes. You can also use 5-gallon buckets with a lid, large grain or rice bags, or dry bags for holding your garbage. Bring extra-tough trash compacter bags for garbage; these won't rip when you transfer garbage from one container to another and allow you to compress the garbage with your foot to maximize space.

It's a good idea to get rid of excess packaging on food before your trip so you don't end up having to deal with lots of waste on the river. If you have a fire, you can burn paper products.

Bring along a mallet or use a rock to flatten aluminum and tin cans, as well as other recyclables, so they are easier to store as you move down river. Having a "thinnest can competition" can motivate kids—and kids at heart—to smash cans down for you. Cans can be transported in an old dry bag, an empty ammo can, or rice or grain sacks.

FIRE PANS

Popular rivers require the use of fire pans and often restrict or forbid the collection of firewood. Make sure you know the rules. If you do have fires, you'll need to pack your ashes out. Fires are great to hang out around, or for cooking with a Dutch oven.

To help keep camps clean for other river runners, most permitted rivers require the use of fire pans.

SPECIALIZED RIVER GEAR

Thousands of people go on multiday raft trips every year, and over time the equipment they use has become quite specialized. Today's river tables tend to be long and narrow so they strap on top of dry boxes or directly onto frames to make seats for passengers; river stoves fold in half to fit inside dry boxes; and the foot pumps employed for hand-washing allow for easy-to-use, hands-free cleaning to help prevent the spread of disease. These are just a few of the tools used on rivers that are not commonly found in other camping settings.

Despite this, it's still amazing how much variety and individualization you'll find in the way people rig their boats and the equipment they choose to bring.

That said, there are definite advantages to purchasing camping gear designed for and by river runners. It just fits together better, and has special features that boost performance in a river setting.

A number of reputable manufacturers make river gear. NRS, Cascade River Gear, and Partner Steel are a few that come to mind for essentials such as toilet systems, tables, frames, dry boxes, and more. You may also be able to find used gear with some online searching. Dry boxes, frames, and toilets tend to be indestructible, especially when handled with care, and buying them used is usually a pretty safe bet.

Costumes, theme nights, and games

Long river trips are good excuses to indulge your inner whimsy. You're alone with your friends on a remote beach far from watchful eyes—what better time for a silly dance party or a costume night? Not all groups are into this kind of thing, but if yours is, plant the seed before the trip so people can bring props.

Theme nights can range from formal affairs, where people wear long gowns and ties, to evenings where you dress like someone else on your trip, to a Mexican piñata party complete with margaritas and sombreros. Thrift stores are great places to find costumes for your trip. A feather boa or a pair of suspenders can do wonders to accessorize your regular river attire and transform boring into amazing.

Some groups like to have cocktail nights, with a theme cocktail for each evening. You can bring a hand-cranked blender to make frozen drinks or a shaker

Long river trips are a great excuse to indulge your inner whimsy and have fun.

Ammo can tug-of-war is a classic beach game rafters use to keep themselves entertained.

RIVER GAMES

Tug-of-war: Grab two small ammo cans and set them in the sand 20 to 30 feet apart. Stack the bow line or a throw rope from one of your rafts in the middle with the ends at the cans. One person stands on each can with the end of the rope in his or her hand. At the signal, they begin pulling the rope in as fast as they can. Once the rope is tight, the goal is to pull your opponent off the ammo can.

Kubb: You can buy this Scandinavian game online. The game involves throwing wooden blocks at other blocks to knock them over.

Beer box pick-up: Take an empty cardboard box from a case of beer or soda and tear off one end. Set the box up tall in the sand. Players must balance on one foot with their hands behind their backs and pick up the box with their teeth. After each player has succeeded, tear the box down an inch and repeat until only one person is left standing.

KanJam: You can buy KanJam online. The game is played with flying discs and a partner, and involves scoring points by hitting the can or goal.

Bocce ball: This game involves throwing colored balls around the beach to see who can get closest to the target. You can buy bocce balls online. Look for glow-in-the-dark balls to add excitement to your game.

Slackline: Take a long piece of tubular webbing (you'll probably need 50 feet or so) and anchor it about a foot off the ground between two trees or boulders. The line has to be as taut as possible, so you'll need to tie it off with a trucker's hitch or something that you can crank down on to create tension. The object is to balance and walk on the line. It's an excellent workout and fun for all ages, but it's hard. You can use a stick or a shoulder to help you get started.

for a good old-fashioned martini. Parties don't have to revolve around alcohol. If you have kids along, make s'mores or play a game that everyone can join in. Bring a *How to Host a Murder* game for a long evening of intrigue, or carry a hand-cranked ice cream maker for an extra special river treat.

Beach games are always popular. Bocce ball, KanJam, Frisbee, croquet, or other games that can be packed up and put in a dry box on the raft for transporting can keep you entertained onshore for hours. Or bring along cards, dice, or a cribbage board if you expect bad weather and lots of tent time.

Music

If you have musicians in your group, have them bring their instruments on the trip. There's nothing quite like sitting around the campfire singing songs while someone plays a guitar. Backpacking guitars are easier to fit into dry boxes, but if you are creative you can find a safe place to carry a full-size guitar on your raft. Other instruments are also fun to have. In addition, many people like to bring speakers and some way to play music on river trips. That's fine as long as you recognize that there are times when people may prefer to enjoy the sounds of nature more than Led Zeppelin. Be considerate—especially if there are other groups camped nearby.

If you have musicians in your group, have them bring their instruments. Making music together on the river can be extra special.

CHAPTER SEVEN
PERSONAL CAMPING GEAR

In addition to the group and river gear, you'll need your own personal equipment for a multiday river trip. At first planning and packing all this stuff can be daunting, but you'll get used to it.

If this is your first multiday river trip, start with a checklist. You can use the one provided in this book, or ask your friends if they have a list you can borrow. I like to store my list on my computer so I can make notes, and add or subtract items as I discover what works best. Plus, the list is easy to find when it's time to pack for my next excursion.

Again, you have the option of going light to minimize weight and maximize space on your rafts, or you can be decadent and bring lots of stuff. I like to go for the middle ground. It's nice to have a few extras—I pack baby wipes, a sundress, and UGGs for example—but don't overdo it. Remember you have to lug that stuff up and down the beach every day, not to mention the extra drag it puts on the boat if everyone is carrying lots of luxuries. A heavy raft is a sluggish raft, which can make it hard to keep up with other rafts on the river, hard to navigate through rapids, and hard for newer rafters to row. If you haven't been on a river trip before, start light. You can add more to your packing list as you gain experience.

TENTS

On most river trips people bring their own personal shelters. This gets a bit crazy if you have fifteen solo travelers in your group. If that's the case you should probably team up to avoid having fifteen tents dotting the shoreline at every camp. But if you are in groups of families or couples, you'll probably have the family groups and couples sharing tents.

On summer trips many rafters opt to sleep out under the stars, either on their boats or onshore.

On summer river trips you may spend most of your nights out under the stars on the beach, but if the wind comes up, the weather turns bad, or there are a lot of bugs, it's important to have a tent. Lightweight summer tents with mosquito netting are nice except when it's sandy and super windy. The lighter particles of sand get blown under the fly and filter down through the netting, leaving you covered in a layer of dust. If you anticipate lots of wind on your trip—Desolation Gray Canyons on the Green River are notorious for wind for example—a four-season tent with ripstop nylon interior walls will help keep out the dust.

Otherwise, your camping gear isn't going to be that different from any other camping trip. Like any overnight excursion into the wilderness, you want to anticipate possible weather conditions and pack accordingly.

A tent is nice to get away from the bugs, off the dirt, and out of the rain.

Here's a sample gear list to get you started.

Personal Gear Checklist

Gear	Warm-Weather Trip	Cold-Weather Trip
1–3 dry bags	Usually you can fit all your gear, minus your tent, in one large dry bag (~70 liter). Use a second smaller dry bag or a large group dry bag for tents. A small day bag is also nice for extra layers, snacks, lip balm, etc.	Same as for warm weather trips, although your bags may need to be bigger to accommodate bulkier stuff
Small ammo or Pelican waterproof box	You can use a small waterproof box to store electronics, cameras, maps, toiletries, etc.	Same

Gear	Warm-Weather Trip	Cold-Weather Trip
Tent	Three-season tent with rain fly and ground cloth (ground cloths are great for sleeping out on the beach). You may also want to consider a fly or hammock if the weather is guaranteed to be mild.	Four-season tent with rain fly
Upper body	1 synthetic base layer (mid- or lightweight)	2 synthetic or wool base layers (light or midweight), one for in camp and the other a "wet set" for on the raft
	1 lightweight fleece, wool jacket, or down sweater	1 insulating layer (down or synthetic-filled, or heavyweight fleece jacket) with hood
		1 down or fleece vest, or an expedition-weight top (optional)
	1 rain jacket	1 rain jacket
	1–2 cotton T-shirts and a sun shirt	1 T-shirt
	1 synthetic sport bra or top (women)	1 synthetic sport bra or top (women)
	1–2 bathing suits	
Lower body	1 pair synthetic or wool long underwear bottoms	2 pairs synthetic or wool long underwear bottoms (mid or lightweight) one "dry" pair for camp; one "wet" pair for the boat
	1 lightweight pair of synthetic pants or jeans for hiking or wearing around camp, protection from thorns, poison ivy, bugs, and cold weather	1 pair insulated pants or shelled polypropylene
	1 pair rain pants	1 pair rain pants
	1–2 pairs quick-dry shorts	
Extras	Loose fitting sundress, skirt, sarong, or trousers (like scrubs)	
Head layers	1 visor or sun hat. Wide brims are useful if they have a chinstrap.	1 visor or sunhat

Gear	Warm-Weather Trip	Cold-Weather Trip
	1 lightweight wool or fleece hat (nice if it fits under your helmet)	1 midweight wool or fleece hat
	1 polypropylene neck gaiter or Buff that can be used for sun protection, etc.	1 neck gaiter or Buff, scarf, or balaclava
		1 fuzzy helmet liner
	1 bandanna (optional)	1 bandanna (optional)
Underwear	2–3 pairs. Technical fabrics work best for quick drying. Shorts with liners work well for men.	2–3 pairs. Technical fabrics work best for quick drying. Shorts with liners work well for men.
Hand layers	1 lightweight pair gloves (wool or synthetic)	1–2 lightweight pairs gloves (wool or synthetic)
	1 pair cotton or nylon "rigging" or rowing gloves	1 pair of insulated gloves or mittens, preferably waterproof or neoprene
Feet layers	2–3 pairs wool or synthetic socks	3 pairs wool or synthetic socks
	Boating shoes, neoprene booties, or strap-on sandals. On sandy rivers your boat shoes will rub, so it may be nice to wear them with a pair of neoprene socks.	Boating shoes and/or boots such as BOGS, fishing boots, or neoprene booties
	1 pair lightweight camp shoes like Crocs, sandals, or slippers	1 pair insulated booties or camp shoes
	1 pair hiking shoes, depending on the trip and the potential for day hiking	1 pair hiking shoes, depending on the trip and the potential for day hiking
Boating gear	PFD, helmet	PFD, helmet
	Throw rope, whistle, knife	Throw rope, whistle, knife
	Dry suit, wet suit, or paddling attire	Dry suit
		Neoprene gloves, mittens, or pogies
Sleeping gear	1 sleeping pad. Paco pads are popular on raft trips. If you have an inflatable sleeping pad, be sure someone in your group has a repair kit.	1 sleeping pad. Paco pads are popular on raft trips. If you have an inflatable sleeping pad, be sure someone in your group has a repair kit.

Gear	Warm-Weather Trip	Cold-Weather Trip
	1 sleeping bag or a quilt and sheet (weight and temperature dependent)	1 sleeping bag, rating determined by expected weather conditions
	1 pillow or pillowcase that can be stuffed with clothes for a pillow	1 pillow or pillowcase that can be stuffed with clothes for a pillow
Toiletries	Toothbrush, toothpaste, comb or brush, unwaxed dental floss with needle for emergency sewing repairs, personal hygiene products, contact lens solution, sunscreen, lip balm, etc. Hand/body lotion is useful on desert rivers, where your skin can really dry out.	Toothbrush, toothpaste, comb or brush, unwaxed dental floss with needle for emergency sewing repairs, personal hygiene products, contact lens solution, sunscreen, lip balm, etc.
	1–2 1-liter water bottles or Camelbak	1–2 1-liter water bottles or Camelbak
Extras	Sunglasses with retaining strap for river use	Sunglasses with retaining strap for river use
	Pee bottle or bucket	Pee bottle or bucket
	Money, credit card, driver's license	Money, credit card, driver's license
	Book, notebook, pencil or pen or ultrafine Sharpie for marking river maps (optional)	Book, notebook, pencil or pen (optional)
	Journal, watercolors (optional)	Journal, watercolors (optional)
	Headlamp	Headlamp
	Lighter or matches packed in a waterproof bag or container	Lighter or matches packed in a waterproof bag or container
	Camera (optional)	Camera (optional)
	Binoculars (optional)	Binoculars (optional)
	Spare batteries for all electronic devices, or consider a portable solar-panel recharger	Spare batteries for all electronic devices, or consider a portable solar-panel recharger
	Fishing rod, tackle, flies or lures (optional)	
		Thermos (optional)

RIVER WEAR

Rafting is wet. You'll get splashed moving through whitewater, not to mention that there's always the possibility of a swim if you get ejected from your raft or flip. Rafters need to gauge their attire according to the air and water temperature.

Your choices run from a bathing suit and shorts, to rain gear or a paddling jacket and pants, to a wet suit or dry suit. A bathing suit is fine in the middle of summer when the temperatures are high, the water warm, and you are confident you aren't going to get caught out in a thunderstorm. Rain gear or a paddling jacket and pants work if you are running easy water, temperatures are mild, and your chance of swimming is minimal. Beware: If you do swim, rain pants can drag you down in the water. For cold conditions, you should wear a wet or dry suit to be safe and comfortable.

As mentioned earlier in this book, the American Canoeing Association considers cold-water conditions to be any water that is less than 60 degrees Fahrenheit, or when the combined air and water temperature is less than 120 degrees Fahrenheit. In these conditions, swimmers rapidly lose their ability to function as they succumb to the cold and become hypothermic.

The proper attire for rafting depends on the air and water temperature. These rafters are sporting various options for staying warm and relatively dry in cooler temperatures.

In hot conditions you may opt to raft in shorts and a bathing suit.

Unprotected by any kind of insulation, you are subject to the 1-10-1 rule when immersed in cold water. This means that during that first minute in the water you'll be incapacitated by cold-water shock, as the cold receptors in your skin respond to the sudden decrease in temperature by evoking uncontrolled gasping, hyperventilation, increased heart rate, and vasoconstriction. Those reactions will pass, so stay calm. Panicking increases the chance you will aspirate water. Instead, take a few seconds to relax and take stock of your situation.

Once the initial shock has passed, you have 10 minutes of functional movement before you lose control of your muscles and can no longer swim or pull yourself out of the water. You then have an hour before you are likely to lose consciousness from hypothermia—if you don't drown before that. Insulation gives you more time to withstand the cold water's effects on your body and, therefore, can save your life.

For cold-water rafting, you need to decide between a paddling jacket and pants, a dry suit or a wet suit. Dry suits are made from waterproof, breathable material, like GORE-TEX, that is sealed at the wrists and neck by rubber gaskets and with either gaskets at the ankles or waterproof socks to keep moisture out. Underneath the suit, you stay dry even if you swim, and can layer clothing according to the air temperature. Wet suits are made from neoprene, which traps a thin layer of water next to your skin. Your body heats up this water and keeps you warm.

Paddling jackets usually have neoprene or rubber wrist and neck closures to keep splashing water out. Paddling pants have neoprene closures at the ankle, although some include built-in socks as well. For rivers where a swim is unlikely but you want to stay dry in the raft, paddling clothes work great. Plus, they are a lot cheaper than a dry suit.

Dry suits

Dry suits are expensive and can be fragile and bulky, but if you plan to boat in cold places they are worth every dollar and ounce, as most of us are more comfortable—and safer—if we are warm and dry.

Your dry suit is going to be one of your most expensive pieces of equipment, with prices ranging from $600 to more than $1,000. If you are investing that kind of money, it's important to make sure you pick a dry suit that is comfortable and durable.

Here are some key things to consider in your purchase:

Material: Dry suits take a lot of wear and tear. Just sitting in your boat causes your suit to rub as you twist and turn with each stroke. Find a dry suit that is durable and that comes with a lifetime warranty. GORE-TEX is the material of choice, but some brands are being made with other materials. If you opt for a different material, read performance reviews online.

Fit: Dry suits, in and of themselves, do not keep you warm; they keep you dry. To be warm you need to wear layers of insulating gear. Just what you wear depends on the air temperature, so you want a suit that is roomy enough to put on multiple layers of clothing underneath and still lets you twist and turn to paddle or row. Many boaters think Kokatat makes the best dry suit on the market, but other brands are catching up and each of them comes with a slightly different fit, so you may find Kokatat is not the best option for you.

Dry suits have rubber gaskets at the hands and neck (and sometimes the ankles) that prevent water from leaking in, so you are warm and dry inside. They are the ultimate way to stay comfortable in cold conditions, but are expensive and challenging to get into and out of.

Try on different models while wearing the layers you anticipate boating in to make sure you are buying a dry suit that is well matched to your physique.

Socks: It's worth investing in a dry suit that comes with built-in socks. The rubber gaskets on dry suits are their weakest link, so if you can minimize the number by eliminating them at your ankles, you'll be happier. Plus, built-in socks allow you to wear cozy wool socks on your feet, which will keep you warmer. Most rafters then wear some kind of boating shoe over the dry suit socks. If you wear a pair of neoprene socks over your dry suit socks, you'll help protect the fabric and prevent pinholes that can lead to leaks. Remember, if you are wearing socks under dry suit socks *and* a pair of neoprene socks over them, your foot is going to be a size or two bigger than normal, so plan accordingly.

Relief zippers: Most dry suits are one-piece suits that look like some kind of space suit. Higher-end suits come in men's and women's models featuring strategically placed zippers that allow you to pee and poop without having to remove the entire dry suit. While it is cheaper to buy dry suits without relief zippers, you'll soon find the extra cost to be worth it. Keep these zippers clean. Dirt causes them to gunk up and malfunction. Don't yank on a stuck zipper. Clean and lube it with some kind of zipper lube, like McNett Zip Tech.

You can also find two-piece dry suits. In the past these suits weren't particularly waterproof on long swims, but Kokatat's Idol is joined by a waterproof zipper that is reputed to be totally watertight. Two-piece dry suits have the advantage of being easier to get into and out of, and you can wear just the top or bottom if it's warm out. Plus, you don't have to use a relief zipper to go to the bathroom. The costs are about the same for a one- or two-piece suit, so it's worth considering a two-piece if you are in the market.

Wet suits

Wet suits are a cheaper option than dry suits, but tend to be less useful in a raft than in kayaks or inflatables, where you are in the water more than in the air. You need to wear a full-body, long-sleeved neoprene suit combined with a paddling jacket and pants to block out the wind and cut down on convective heat loss if you are sitting on a raft in cold, wet conditions. Wet suits also take longer to dry than dry suits. For these reasons, you may as well opt for a dry suit if your goals include cold-water rafting. Wet suits are quite a bit cheaper, however, and if that is what you have, it's much better than nothing.

Where wet suits really shine is in milder conditions, where you would just steam in your juices inside a dry suit. There are a variety of options for wet suits that keep you comfortable in warmer climes: farmer johns, shortie suits, Hydro-Skins, neoprene shirts and shorts, etc. For summer boating, these options tend to be lighter, more packable, and cheaper (costing between $100 to $400) than a dry suit.

As with all boating gear, you'll preserve the life of your neoprene if you take care of it. Rinse your wet suit in fresh water at the end of the day and hang it up to dry away from direct sunlight. Once you get home at the end of a trip, wash the suit in warm water with a mild soap to remove body oils and dirt. Rinse and dry the wet suit thoroughly, and store it in a cool, dry place away from the sun. If your wet suit or other neoprene product becomes funky and smelly, you can buy special soaps that kill bacteria and funguses.

ACCESSORIES

Neoprene socks or booties, gloves, mittens, and pogies

In addition to wet suits, neoprene socks, gloves, mittens, or pogies can be useful tools for staying warm in a wet environment.

In a dry suit with built-in socks, neoprene socks or booties are unnecessary. In a paddling suit or wet suit, they help keep your feet warm during the day. Look for socks that fit snugly and can be worn under your boat shoes. If you opt for neoprene booties, make sure they fit easily over your dry suit, if you are wearing one. Another trick is to wear GORE-TEX socks over wool or fleece socks. The GORE-TEX will keep water out and your feet dry.

The choice between gloves, pogies, or mittens depends on your personal preference, the ambient air temperature, and the type of boating you plan to do. In general, gloves are the least warm option, but they give you the most dexterity so you can perform delicate tasks without having to take them off.

These rafters are ready for cold weather, wearing dry suits, gloves, and hats under their helmets.

RIGGING GLOVES

Loading, unloading, rigging, and rowing are hard on your hands. In addition to having gloves to keep warm, many rafters opt to wear a lightweight pair of gloves while working around or rowing the raft. You can buy specialized gloves for rowing or pick up a pair of nylon work gloves at the hardware store. If you want to wear work gloves for rowing, look for something with a grippy palm.

Gloves

Too-tight gloves will constrict blood flow and make your fingers cold. Nylon coverings on the glove's palms make it hard to grip your oars. Nylon coverings on the back of the hand protect the neoprene from tears, but increase evaporative cooling and so make the glove a bit colder.

Mittens

Mittens are warmer than gloves, but you won't be able to do anything that requires dexterity without taking them off, and it can be cumbersome to deal with the on-off routine if you anticipate making lots of adjustments. Lobster-claw mittens are a compromise. They give you a more agility than mittens and more warmth than gloves.

Pogies

Pogies are designed to slide over your oar, allowing you to hold the handle with your bare skin while giving you protection from the wind and rain. Pogies don't work on raft paddles. Pogies tend to be the warmest option out there, especially when worn with neoprene gloves underneath.

Boating shoes

Lots of rafters boat in strap-on sandals or neoprene booties, but you may want to consider boat shoes, such as those made by Astral, if you are going to spend a lot of time on the river. Boat shoes protect your feet better than sandals, and if you wear them with neoprene socks, you're less likely to have rubbing from sand caught in sandal straps. Boat shoes aren't as clammy as neoprene booties (unless, of course, you are wearing neoprene socks!) and you can hike in them.

There are all kinds of shoes that work for boating, from strap-on sandals to water shoes and mesh sneakers. You want something with a grippy sole that keeps your feet from slipping on wet rocks and slick rafts.

If you opt for boat shoes, look for the following:

- Shoes that are comfortable, supportive, and lightweight
- Shoes made from nonabsorbing, quick-drying, durable fabric. Avoid so-called waterproof shoes. No shoe is waterproof if you submerge it in water. Waterproof coatings tend to just trap water inside.
- Shoes with sticky rubber soles that provide traction as well as protection and cushioning
- Shoes with a secure lacing system
- Shoes that are roomy enough to go over dry suit booties and socks or neoprene socks. You can also opt to pull the insoles out of your shoes so you have extra space to fit your shoes over your dry suit and a warm pair of socks.

PERSONAL SAFETY EQUIPMENT

You need to carry some basic rescue equipment if you plan to raft whitewater. Remember, carrying safety gear is useless if you don't know how to use it. If you intend to tackle whitewater, it's wise to take a swiftwater rescue course or to practice basic rescue techniques on your own. We will go into more detail on basic rescue later in this book.

Each individual on your trip should carry a whistle. It's best if the whistle is stored where you can get to it quickly, especially if you are in the water. A lot of people like to hang a whistle from the zipper pull of their PFD, but there's a risk in this. The weight of the whistle can pull down on the zipper, causing it to open. It's better to put the whistle on a short piece of accessory cord and tie it to the shoulder strap of your PFD. Whistles are used to sound an alarm when something goes wrong, such as when a raft flips or gets pinned, or someone is in the water. You can also use the whistle to get someone's attention when a group is too spread out on the water.

This rafter has a knife, a whistle, a rescue PFD, and a webbing line, complete with a couple of carabiners, around his waist so he's ready for just about anything.

In addition to a whistle, lots of boaters carry a river knife. River knives allow you to extract yourself if you get entangled in a rope or pinned in your raft. Again, the knife has to be handy to be useful, and you need to know how to use one correctly to keep it from being a liability. Most river knives come with a way to be attached to the outside of your PFD.

In remote areas it is also a good idea to carry a lighter and some fire starter in a small sealed plastic bag in one of your pockets. This way, if you somehow become separated from your equipment, you can start a fire to get warm. I also carry a lightweight garbage bag in my pocket that I can use as an emergency rain jacket in a pinch.

THE LITTLE EXTRAS THAT MAKE A DIFFERENCE

Experienced river-goers all have special items they bring along that make life on the river just a little bit better. Gear lists can be pretty vague. After all, when the list says pants, it begs the question of what kind of pants? And it says nothing about what will feel good after a long hot day in the sun—or the reverse, a long cold day in the rain.

A well-seasoned river rat knows just what to bring to be comfortable and entertained regardless of the weather.

Just the Right Clothing

The key on a river trip is to wear clothes that dry quickly and help you stay cool or warm depending on the weather conditions. Comfort is important, and for that you may find a flowy sundress, yoga pants, or loose-fitting cotton trousers feel awesome after spending all day in a soggy bathing suit or wet suit. Many people—male and female alike—like to wear a sarong tied like a skirt around camp. Sarongs are versatile, cool, comfy, and can also be used for sun protection on the raft or for some extra privacy when you want to make a quick change on the beach. Plus, they let you air out if you've been trapped in wet neoprene all day.

As for your feet, you'll probably be wearing some kind of river shoe, river sandal, or neoprene bootie on the raft during the day. When you get to camp, you'll be psyched to get out of those soggy shoes as quickly as possible. Flip-flops make great easy camp shoes that you can slip on and off with ease. Or you may want to consider a pair of slippers with a sole that you can wear around camp for extra comfort and warmth. If you plan to do a lot of hiking, bring hiking shoes, and for wet, cold trips a pair of rubber boots or waders can help keep your feet warm and dry, especially when you are loading and unloading your raft.

Finally, have a little flair on the river. It's fun to be yourself and dress up at night. It's also important to do what you need to be comfortable and healthy.

It's nice to have loose, flowy cotton clothing to wear in camp after you've been trapped in wet clothes all day long on the raft.

SKIN CARE

If you are going on a Grand Canyon or any desert river trip, be prepared for your skin to get trashed if you don't take care of it. The sand, sun, water, and wind do incredible damage if you aren't diligent. That includes painful cracks and raw spots from rubbing on your hands and feet. Bring along a thick, viscous moisturizing cream, such as CeraVe Moisturizing Cream, Super Salve, climbOn, or Eucerin Intensive Repair Cream, for all-body moisturizing. In addition, consider bringing Bag Balm, Burt's Bees hand salve, or Vaseline for cracks in your hands and feet. If you do develop cracks, Super Glue helps close them and reduces pain.

Some people carry lightweight cotton gardening gloves to sleep in. They'll slather cream or bag balm on their hands, put on the gloves, and go to bed. Likewise, wearing socks to sleep can help prevent cracking in your feet, as does wearing shoes and socks around camp or on the raft.

Toiletries

River trips can be rough on your skin. Often it's hard to escape the sun and you're usually covered in sand. For that reason there are a few items that can make you feel a lot more comfortable at the end of the day, such as baby wipes, packaged cleaning cloths, or facial cleansing pads to wipe away the grime and sunscreen. Bring along a plastic grocery bag to hold used wipes. They shouldn't go in the groover. After cleansing with a wipe it's nice to follow up with a thorough dousing in some kind of a thick, scentless moisturizing lotion.

Hair

River guides with long hair recommend carrying a small bottle of leave-in conditioner to help deal with tangles. Plus, they bring lots of hair ties and headbands, and a fun hat that lets them express themselves as well as block out the sun.

Hygiene

It's important to think about cleanliness on the river, and not just about keeping your hands washed. If you are sitting around in damp clothes all day, it's easy for

MENSTRUATION

Managing your period on the river isn't a big deal, but it helps to be prepared. Pack a little feminine hygiene kit in a ziplock bag that contains tampons and/or pads, and a trash bag for used products. I like to use a plastic grocery bag that is opaque and hides what's inside. You may also want to include single-use feminine cleansing cloths in your kit. Used items can be put in the group garbage container.

things to get a bit rank down in your nether regions. If it's warm outside, jump into the river whenever you can, and when you get to camp change into dry, loose-fitting cotton clothes to give yourself a breather. Ladies might want to bring along a cotton bandanna that can be used as a pee rag for wiping after urination. That sounds gross, but the truth is you are only wiping away a few drops of urine, and you can rinse the bandanna off in the river whenever you want.

It's important to keep yourself clean and dry to avoid yeast infections or other discomfort. Fellows need to be careful about that too, so everyone benefits from washing their privates regularly while on the river. Soap isn't necessary for daily rinses, but you may want to bring along biodegradable soap or shampoo for an occasional bath, especially on longer trips. Check river regulations to find out where the land managers want soap disposed of. Some river managers want you to bathe above the high-water mark; others say to put everything—including soap—in the river.

Books, journals, painting supplies

On most river trips, you'll find yourself with lots of time on your hands. I like to bring an e-reader stocked with books to keep me entertained. Some people enjoy journaling. Others bring along travel-size watercolor sets to paint with. Natural history guides, flower or bird books, and binoculars are all great tools for learning about and exploring the environment around you as you float downstream.

If you are traveling through the land of scorpions, such as in the Grand Canyon, bring a black light so you can go scorpion hunting at night. Scorpions turn neon green under a black light! But remember: Look; don't touch.

A portable watercolor set and journal allow you to tap into your creative side on the river.

Sleeping in style

Most river rats opt to sleep on Paco pads, but any inflatable camping mattress will provide a soft bed during your trip. In addition, if you are on a summer trip where the nights are hot, you may want to bring along a sheet and a quilt rather than a sleeping bag. Some people include a pillow for the ultimate luxury, but if you want to save space, you can bring a pillowcase or use a T-shirt stuffed with jackets and other soft clothing to make a good headrest. Finally, an oversized ground cloth or polypropylene mat keeps you off the ground and out of the sand.

If you are in a big group, you may want to consider bringing earplugs to help yourself sleep. You can usually spread out on the beach and get some privacy, but if there are snorers or late-night talkers on your team, it's nice to be able to tune them out.

Many rafters never bother to set up a tent on river trips, opting instead to sleep out under the stars.

With a big ground cloth and a thick Paco pad, just about any place makes a good bedroom.

And don't forget to bring a container to pee in if you don't want to have to go down to the river in the middle of the night. Women often like a small bucket with a wide-mouth, such as a yogurt container; men can go for a wide-mouth water bottle.

CHAPTER EIGHT
FOOD

There are as many ways to organize the cooking and menu planning on your trip as there are people. Everyone has a system or a variation on a system that they think is the absolute best. Realistically all of them work. The important thing is organization. If everyone understands how the meals are going to work, no one goes hungry.

You probably won't lose weight on a river trip as the food is usually good and plentiful, plus you can always eat cake.

One of the simplest ways to figure out your food is to hire an outfitter to plan, prep, and pack all of your meals. When you go this route, you usually end up with bags or boxes of food organized by day with preparation instructions included. This system works great, but it's not the cheapest route to take.

Another system is to create cook teams responsible for planning and preparing a certain number of meals during the trip. How you organize your schedule is up to you. Some people like to have one team do all the meals on one day. Some people like to have a team start with dinner and go through lunch the following day. Some people like to do group breakfasts and dinner and have individuals bring their own lunches. Regardless of how you line out your system, make sure to communicate the plan to your group well before the trip so people can come up with their menus. If you intend to cook as a group, make sure everyone is aware of any food allergies or preferences and lets the rest of the group know what they are cooking so you don't all end up making the same thing.

If you are going the "everything but the kitchen sink" way, you can bring frozen food and fresh produce to help diversify your menu. The goal is to have

Rafting with big coolers and lots of ice allows you to enjoy fresh produce and meat throughout your river trip.

ICE OR NO ICE?

You can do a multiday river trip without bringing along a cooler. It just means shifting your menu toward a backpacking-style plan—focusing on dried food and staples—rather than the standard river fare with all its bells and whistles. Without a cooler you leave behind fresh produce, meat, and cold beverages, but you'll save on space and weight, which can be advantageous, especially on long trips with lots of technical boating.

You can also plan for the latter half of a long trip to be "iceless," and shift your menu from fresh foods to freeze-dried or dehydrated options once you use up the perishable stuff.

Some people treat ice as a kind of science project. They may go so far as to order "sculpture ice" or "poured ice" from an ice provider. Sculpture and poured ice has fewer air bubbles in it than regular ice, and should last longer. Ice aficionados may have access to a walk-in cooler that allows them to freeze a layer of ice on the bottom of their cooler prior to the trip. High-quality coolers tend to seal better than cheap ones, and, therefore, hold ice longer. If you can't afford to drop several hundred dollars on a cooler, good cooler management (see page 159) will help you preserve your ice.

sufficient quantity and variety for everyone on the trip. People need to be well fed to avoid food stress, which can put a damper on any outdoor adventure. The amount of time and energy you want to put into your meals depends on your river. If you anticipate long days on the water, simple foods are preferable. Short days with lots of camp time allow you more flexibility for creativity and complexity.

If you are looking to travel as lightly as possible, consider dehydrated foods, one-pot meals, and concentrated foods such as energy bars, cheeses, and preserved meats like salami. Borrow ideas from backpackers to help lighten your load and minimize your space needs. The advantage to going light is that you need fewer rafts, less propane for cooking, and your rafts will be lighter and more maneuverable in rapids.

If you want to go light, bring a backpacking stove with a small pot and freeze-dried or dehydrated food so you can leave the coolers, elaborate kitchen setups, and big propane tanks behind.

FOOD SERVICE SAFETY

A river trip can turn into a nightmare if everyone ends up sick from improper food preparation and care. This is not something to be taken lightly. There have been times when sick river runners have contaminated camps along a river, so cleanliness is critical. Make sure to set up a hand-washing station near the toilet facilities so it's easy to wash up after you use the bathroom. Hand-washing before food preparation and eating is also critical.

In camp, be sure food is stored properly to avoid encounters with rodents, insects, bees, bears, and other animals. Dry boxes and coolers with animal-proof clasps are critical to keep your food and the animals safe. If you are in bear country, you may want to bring bearproof canisters or barrels.

Clean and sanitize dishes after every use.

If you have group snacks that come in a big container, have people pour the snacks into their hands rather than dig in to grab some. This helps keep dirty hands out of group food.

TIPS FOR PACKING AND CONSERVING FOOD

- Freeze premade meals, meat, milk, and other fresh items at home. Frozen pasta sauces, lasagnas, curries etc., can be reheated in a skillet or Dutch oven.
- Bring hardier produce, such as kale versus spinach, or apples versus bananas.
- Use block ice and place an insulating piece of EVA foam or Reflectix over your food inside the cooler. Place a wet towel or an insulating cover on the outside to help keep the cooler cold. Avoid opening and closing the cooler repeatedly. Plan what you need to get out of the cooler and get it all in one go.
- Drain the cooler daily, as ice melts more rapidly when sitting in water. Also, draining keeps your foods from getting soggy if there are pinholes in your freezer bags.
- For long trips you may want to consider using dry ice in the cooler that holds items for the end of the journey.
- Crack eggs into a plastic water bottle or a heavy-duty plastic bag and freeze before the trip to avoid having to deal with fragile eggshells, and to serve as yet another chunk of "ice" in your cooler. Or, if you prefer, eggs can be stored in your dry box. Egg trays—usually holding 20–30 eggs apiece—stack snugly in dry boxes. Paper trays can be cut to fit if the size isn't quite right.
- Use food that can spoil early in the trip (this includes fresh veggies, lettuce, bread, etc).
- If space is at a premium, bring flat breads and crackers instead of regular bread.
- Try to plan portions to avoid lots of leftovers.
- Talk to your group to see if things can be shared to avoid duplication, such as condiments, drinks, etc.
- Fresh fruit is more likely to be eaten if you cut it into pieces. If you plan on apples for lunch, cut them up so people actually consume them.
- Turn produce regularly in the cooler to help preserve it. Sitting directly on ice or in meltwater will damage produce, so you need to move it around to keep it from spoiling.
- When pulling produce for a meal, always use the worst-looking stuff first to make sure it is used up and doesn't go bad.
- Dry boxes only stay so dry in the event of a flip. If you are boating a river where flipping is likely, consider waterproofing your dry food in plastic bags inside the dry box.

Dishwashing

River runners typically use a three- or four-basin wash system to ensure all dishes are cleaned and sanitized after every use. Plastic bins, collapsible buckets, or metal "chickie" pails that can be stacked inside each other for storage work well for this system. The advantage of chickie pails is they can be placed directly on the stove or blaster for heating wash water.

To wash your dishes, start by scraping food scraps into the garbage. It's nice to have an extra spatula to help with this task. In a four-basin system, the first basin is used for a prewash, which allows you to get rid of the gunk or scraps that dirty dishwater quickly. This step isn't critical, but some people like it. The next three containers are vital, however.

The first basin in a three-basin system contains warm soapy water for washing. The second basin contains warm or cold rinse water. The third contains cold rinse water with half a capful of bleach to sanitize the dishes. Hot water

Clean, sanitized dishes help ensure that no one gets sick during your trip.

Set up your dishwashing station so it's convenient and easy to use. That way washing is less of a chore for everyone.

deactivates bleach, hence the reason your final rinse must be cold. On clear rivers, you can use river water for dishes. If the river is silty or muddy, it may be best to use jug water, in which case it is important to be conservative but still thorough. Alternately you can pull silty water from the river and let it sit in a bucket until the silt settles out before pouring it into your washing basins.

Make sure to start washing the cleanest dishes first so the dishwater stays cleaner longer. Dishes must be in the bleach water for thirty seconds to be sanitized.

Once the dishes are washed, place them in a mesh drying hammock suspended from a table. The dishes can stay here overnight. If you need to pack up to get on the river, let the dishes air dry as long as possible and then pack them up.

Wastewater is strained through either a metal or cloth strainer, and all remaining food particles collected in the strainer are placed in the garbage. The leftover gray water is either disposed of in the river or above the high-water mark. This decision is determined by the specific river regulations. Water is usually poured into the river on desert or glacial rivers, but is not on clear mountain streams.

Dishwashing can be brutal on your hands, especially on longer river trips. Pack a couple of pairs of dishwashing gloves to protect your skin. Make sure to store the gloves in a dry box overnight so mice don't make holes in them.

RIVER BREAKFASTS

River breakfasts can be cold or hot. The type you choose is largely a reflection of your time constraints. Go with cold on mornings when you want to get out of camp fast, and hot when you have more time.

Cooked breakfasts can include French toast, pancakes, hash browns, or egg sandwiches. You can make things like breakfast burritos at home and heat them up (or eat them cold) on the river for an easy breakfast. Baked goods made before your trip are also popular. You can include meat, such as bacon or sausage. (Cleanup after cooking breakfast meat can be time-consuming, so be sure to factor in time to drain grease and clean greasy pans when having bacon or sausage for your morning meal.)

Hot breakfasts on the river can range from fried eggs to pancakes or French toast.

Cooking on the river is a time to unleash your inner chef.

Breakfast doesn't have to be elaborate. If you anticipate a long day or want to make the food on your trip simple and easy, you can have cereal and fruit for a quick, easy meal.

Cold breakfasts usually involve cereal with milk, yogurt, or a milk substitute like Rice Dream. It's nice to include three or four different types of cereal so people have a choice. Fruit can round out the meal. Melon holds up to packing well but takes up a lot of space. Apples and oranges are also good options for rivers because they tend to withstand travel.

Most breakfasts start with a hot drink, usually coffee, tea, or hot chocolate, so even with cold breakfasts you'll need to boil water.

RIVER LUNCHES

Lunches can be a formal affair, where you pull out a table and make an elaborate meal, or can be simple, where you pack a lunch at breakfast and eat on the fly during the day. Some groups I've traveled with like to have individuals bring their own lunches so they can eat whenever they feel like it as they float down-

On upscale river trips, lunches can be elaborate affairs complete with tablecloths, fresh fruit, cold cuts, cheese, veggies, and dessert.

stream. This works well when everyone is in his or her own raft with access to a cooler and food storage. If your trip includes a lot of kayakers or people in small boats, it's usually easier to do a group lunch, or to have people pack their lunches in the morning after breakfast so they have access to it during the day.

One of the most common river lunches is a sandwich buffet with a variety of breads, cold cuts, sliced cheese, hummus, lettuce (iceberg travels well), tomatoes, pickles, avocados, etc. You can also make chicken or tuna salad, pasta salad, or three-bean salad for some variety. Tortillas are great for making wraps and are a good alternative for lunches later in the trip, when bread may be getting moldy or smashed in the dry boxes. Pringles make a good river snack since they hold up to packing better than bagged chips. Cookies and fruit round out the meal. The key is to offer some variety so people can pick and choose what suits them.

A yummy but basic lunch spread includes cold cuts, cheese, lettuce, tomatoes, avocados, onions, pickles, and bread.

If you want a change from cold cuts, you can have cold salmon, hummus, or chicken salad for lunch.

If you have a long day on the river planned, you can always just eat lunch on the raft. Make sure you put everything you need in a handy place when you load your boat in the morning to expedite your picnic.

If you think you'll be eating a lot of lunches on the go, it's a good idea to pack some plastic containers so you can make your sandwich in camp in the morning and eat it whenever you get hungry during the day.

Make sure to identify any utensils or dishes that you'll need to prepare your lunch, and put them in a special spot before the rafts are packed so they are easy to find when you pull over for lunch.

SNACKS

Have some snacks readily available for people throughout the day. Many groups opt to have individuals bring their own snacks so they have sufficient amounts and options. Energy bars, trail mix, pretzels, gorp, crackers, mixed nuts, and candy can all provide a quick boost on a long day. Have people put their snacks in their day bags so they can get to it without having to open dry boxes or a cooler.

If it's cold, a few insulated bottles for hot drinks can help chilly boaters revive.

Keep some snacks—bars, gorp, crackers, etc.—easily accessible so people, especially kids, can eat when they need some extra calories to get through the day.

RIVER DINNERS

Dinners can also run the gamut from simple to complex. Many rafters bring Dutch ovens so they can bake or make casseroles on the river. Others opt to prepare and freeze a meal at home so all they have to do on the river is reheat it. Weight is generally not a concern unless you are trying to go light or are on a long river trip with a lot of people.

Dutch Ovens

Dutch ovens (DOs) can be used for baking breads, cakes, and casseroles like lasagna, or can be used as a warming dish.

To use a DO for baking, set up your fire pan to heat the coals. You'll need thirty to forty briquettes per DO. Wipe the DO with an oiled paper towel or empty butter wrapper and load it up with whatever you are cooking. Put the lid on securely.

Spread ten to fifteen charcoal briquettes in an even layer in the fire pan and place the DO on top. Using a shovel, stack the rest of the briquettes onto the lid, spreading them out across the top.

TIPS FROM THE PROS

- Use instant rice (white or brown), instant oatmeal, and just-add-water pancake mix for ease of preparation.
- Shredded cheese packages work great for cheesy meals—lasagna, Mexican dishes, etc.—and make preparation faster and tidier.
- Squeezable mayo, mustard, jelly, etc. make lunches easier and require less cleanup. You can refill squeeze bottles from larger containers at home if you want to minimize the packaging.
- Pack a spice kit with commonly used spices for the entire group. This includes oil, salt, pepper, hot sauce, soy sauce, garlic, etc.
- If quantities are short, serve people food to avoid the front of the line taking too much.

Dutch oven lasagna is a special hearty treat that tastes great after a hard day of boating.

Cooking times in the DO will vary depending on what you are preparing. Usually it takes about forty-five minutes for most recipes. You should be able to smell your masterpiece for roughly ten to fifteen minutes before it's ready.

Allow the DO to cool before you wash it. Placing it in cold water when hot causes the metal to warp.

DRINKS

Most groups have people bring their own beverages to ensure everyone has what they want to drink. You don't have to go that route, of course, but it's one way to ensure the one-beer-a-week person doesn't end up having to pay for the six-pack-a-day person's habit. It's also nice to have some nonalcoholic drinks and drink mix to add to your water. Water that sits in warm plastic jugs all day can begin to be bit unpleasant to drink, and it's important to keep everyone hydrated on the river.

If you have the luxury of abundant cooler space, you can devote one to keeping canned drinks cold. Cans can also be put in a drag bag and towed behind the raft to chill.

KEEPING DRINKS COLD

Whether you are drinking beer, soda, or water, it can be hard to keep your beverages cold on the river. Some people like to have a designated drink cooler. When cooler space is at a premium, hang a mesh drag bag off the stern of a raft to keep drinks a bit cooler during the day. It's not like keeping them on ice but it's better than nothing in the heat. You'll want to pull the drag bag into the raft when you go through rapids. In addition, don't forget to pack a drink koozie to help keep your beverage cold while you drink it. If you expect to encounter yellow jackets on your trip, a cup with a lid is nice.

On cold-weather trips, pack a few insulated bottles to hold tea or cocoa for a quick pick-me-up on the river.

WATER

Where you get your drinking, cooking, and washing water depends on the river you are on. On some trips you get by with getting all your water directly from the river (although it should be treated if it's not boiled). On other rivers, you may opt to bring drinking water in 5-gallon jugs and get the rest of your water (for washing and cooking) out of the river. On still other rivers (especially those with a lot of runoff from farms, glacial silt, or sediment) you may want to bring all the water you plan to use—except for washing water—in jugs. Jugs can be refilled from springs or clear side streams as you empty them.

FOOD AMOUNTS

One of the hardest things about planning a river menu is figuring out how much food is enough. It can be helpful to check with your group members before the trip to find out if they consider themselvves to be big eaters, light eaters, or just average. Young children and older people tend to eat a bit less than your average adult. Teens can put down a lot of food, especially teenage boys.

In general, I like to use the serving guidelines on recipes as a starting point and then round up or down based on the composition of my group, as well as the weather conditions and the level of exertion anticipated on the trip. Cold-weather trips typically mean boaters need more calories. Hot-weather trips often call for more drinks, sodas, and fruit.

It's nice to have plenty of food, but having too much is a drag and a waste. Plan your amounts carefully, and if you find the group isn't eating everything you prepare, cut things down to avoid having leftovers to throw away.

SAMPLE FOOD QUESTIONNAIRE

Food Questionnaire for _____ (please insert name)

Check here and send this back if you don't care about the food at all, will eat whatever you are served, and NEVER complain: _____

OR

Please highlight any major food allergies, preferences, or dislikes:

I have an allergy / food intolerance to _____

I have a strong preference to _____

I am a vegetarian: _____

I eat fish: _____

Having vegetables at every dinner is very important to me: _____

If there is one thing that makes me happy it is _____

The one thing that makes me upset or not enjoy a food is _____

Breakfast:

1. Do you want soy milk or 2-percent for your granola? Are you a die-hard half-and-half-in-coffee person?
2. Do you take sugar in hot drinks? Do you use sugar subs and if so, which type?
3. How much coffee / decaf coffee do you drink? Are you bringing your own?
4. Would you prefer tea or cocoa? Are you bringing your own?
5. Any special fruit requests for the days we have fruit?
6. Do you prefer variety for breakfast or are you happy with one set meal (e.g., oatmeal or pancakes)
7. Anything you love for breakfast (e.g., sausages, bacon, chili, or eggs)

Lunch:

1. Would you like lunch meats as well as cheese? If so, which types?
2. Do you like canned tuna or salmon?
3. Do you like pickles?
4. What are your favorite condiments? (e.g., how much do you use mustard, spicy mustard, mayo?)
5. Do you like peanut butter and jelly?
6. Anything you love for variety for lunches?
7. What are your favorite types of chips?
8. Should we bring group snacks or will you bring your own?

Dinner:

☐ 1. I prefer simple meals over complex meals.
☐ 2. Desserts are very important to me.
☐ 3. As a meat eater, I want meat every dinner.
☐ 4. As a vegetarian, I want protein every meal.
☐ 5. Any special dinner ideas / requests?

Courtesy of Rafting the Grand Canyon WIKI (https://rrfw.org/RaftingGrandCanyon)

If you are a meat eater, a steak dinner cooked over the coals can't be beat, but make sure you know your group's dietary preferences before serving meat.

FOOD QUANTITY GUIDELINES

When it comes to how much food people will eat, every group is different. You need to find the balance between having too much food (i.e., leftovers) and not having enough. Remember, your group will start out eating light and then eat more as the trip progresses. Take into account the ages of people in your group (kids eat less), the number of people, boy versus girl ratio, daily activities that may require extra energy, etc.

CHAPTER NINE
A DAY ON THE RIVER

Every day is slightly different on a river trip. You are in a new section of the river corridor so the scenery changes, and the obstacles you confront that day also change, but there's a rhythm to life that is predictable and worth considering as you plan your first multiday trip.

RISE AND SHINE

Most groups opt to have a cook team assigned to the morning kitchen duties. The team's job is to get up, make breakfast (and coffee!), and then clean up and

It's nice to have a designated cook team assigned to get up in the morning to get the coffee going. If you rotate chores through your group, you'll get plenty of days to lie in while your friends start breakfast.

put away the kitchen while the rest of the group packs up their personal stuff. Sometimes you'll also have a designated cleanup crew. If you aren't on the cook or cleanup team, once your gear is loaded and your dry bag is on the beach waiting to go onto a raft, you can sub in for someone on one of those teams so they can deal with their personal stuff.

Mornings go best when the cooks prep a bit the night before so they know where their food is stored and they have a plan for what time they will get going. If people get up early to make you breakfast, it's nice to be respectful and get out of bed to eat when the food is ready. If you want to have a morning to sleep in, that's fine too—just make sure everyone knows so you don't have someone standing in the kitchen at 6 a.m. with a pot of hot coffee and no one to serve.

Loading your dry bags

Today you can find dry bags that seal with a kind of zipper closure (Watershed's patented ZipDry sealing closure or NRS's TIZIP Master Seal waterproof

Dry bags are the standard way to carry your personal camping gear. Make sure to get out the excess air and roll them closed tightly so they are waterproof.

ZIPPERED DRY BAGS

The longer you spend on the river, the more likely you will splurge on a dry bag with a zipper closure that gives you easy access to your stuff. Watershed makes bags that open with what it calls a ZipDry sealing closure, which allows you to get in and out of your bag easily. Rather than having to roll and unroll the opening, you just "unzip" a Watershed bag. NRS and AIRE make dry bags with waterproof zippers as well. These bags tend to be a little expensive, but if you plan to spend a lot of time on the river you may want to consider the investment for their added convenience.

zipper, for example) or ones with the more common roll-top designs. Either type works well for keeping your equipment dry on the raft, but they need to be packed properly to work properly. Most bags seal best when they are full but not overflowing. You can use a big dry bag for carrying your camping gear, clothing, and so forth. Remember you probably won't have access to that bag during the day. Anything you need on the raft should be packed in a small dry bag that serves as a day bag, or in an ammo can that you can get to easily.

Tents may be too big to go in your clothes bag. If you have a spare dry bag in the group, you can put a bunch of tents in one bag. Sometimes people make room for tents in a dry box or large ammo can. If your tent will fit in your personal dry bag, you may want to consider bringing along a trash compacter bag to put it in so if you have to put the tent away wet it won't get other things in your bag damp.

Dry bags pack best if you simply stuff items loosely in so that all the nooks and crannies are filled and you aren't left with lots of awkward spaces in your bag. But this means things are a bit chaotic when you unload in camp. I like to bring a few stuff sacks or duffle bags so I can organize my gear in camp once I unload my dry bag. I pack everything loosely in the bag for the day, but when I'm unpacking at night I have a duffle bag for my clothes and a stuff sack for my sleeping stuff so things aren't exploded all over the place. If you like to use stuff sacks in your dry bag, try to use big stuff sacks packed loosely, so they are compressible rather than rock hard and difficult to fit into small spaces.

At night when I'm sleeping outside the tent, I'll put my belongings back into the dry bag for storage in case there's a shower overnight.

To load a roll-top dry bag, stuff everything down to the bottom, taking time to fill in the voids as you push things in. Once everything is packed, pull the two sides of the bag together and fold the top over once to create a seal. The top of the bag will have a stiff edge, which folds neatly over on itself for this purpose. After the top edge is folded, push down on the bag to force out excess air, then roll the top down carefully, making each roll tight and even. You'll want at least three rolls. Four rolls are better. Push down on the bag. If you hear any air escaping, the bag is not sealed properly or it has a hole. Either way, if air is coming out, water can get in, so figure out why you have a leak.

To finish closing the bag, clip the buckles in place. Bags have different closing systems. The buckles may be on the sides, with a second set of straps going over the top, or the sides of the bags may be folded back on themselves to clip into each other on top.

Pack your small dry bag the same way, but fill it with things you'll need during the day: extra layers, snacks, rain gear etc.

I try to avoid putting anything breakable, leakable, or hard in my dry bags. For these items—sunscreen, e-readers, cameras, etc.—it's nice to have an ammo can or small dry box that you can clip onto the raft. Hard items in your dry bags make holes more likely, and no one likes to have a lotion explosion all over their clothes.

Finally, everyone must have access to a water bottle during the day. You'll need to have a way to clip your bottle onto the raft so it won't get lost if you flip. A 1-foot piece of tubular webbing duct-taped into a loop on the bottle and hooked into the boat with a carabiner works well for a simple clipping system.

Breaking down camp

Start packing up your personal gear while the cooks are making breakfast. When you are done, you can step in to help them finish up in the kitchen.

Breaking down the kitchen is easy if you have a dry box large enough to hold your kitchen supplies in one place. This box can be brought up to camp overnight and returned to its place on the raft in the morning, so you don't have to make repeated visits to the raft to load and unload your kitchen gear. Kitchen boxes tend to be heavy so make sure you have at least two people to move it and take your time, especially if you have to move over rocks.

Once the dishes are dry, take them out of the drying rack, place them in the kitchen box, fold up the drying rack, and load it up. Disconnect the stove from the propane tank, making sure the tank is closed tightly. Place the stove along with the hoses you use to attach it to the propane tank in a dry box where they

While you wait for breakfast to be prepared, start packing up your tents and personal gear so you can help with the group gear after you eat.

are protected from sand and water. Put the propane tank down on the beach for loading into one of the rafts.

Tables should be folded up and moved down to the beach next to the raft where they are stored.

Once everything is packed up and ready to be put on the raft, make a last call for the groover, and then load up the groover and the hand-washing station and place those items on the beach next to the raft that will carry them.

Loading the rafts

Moving gear up and down the beach can be strenuous, and some items are heavy. Don't hurt yourself struggling with a heavy load when you can find someone to help you move it and make the job easier. When camp is back from the shoreline, big groups can make a bucket brigade to pass lighter items up and down from the rafts to the campsite.

Don't throw dry bags around. Tossing a loaded dry bag onto a rocky shore-line is guaranteed to result in holes—if not the first time, then sometime—and a hole means that suddenly all your dry clothes will be wet.

Transporting your gear from camp to the rafts can be strenuous, as some items are heavy and awkward. You can share the load by getting a buddy to help you carry things, especially big items like the kitchen box.

To expedite loading and unloading the rafts, form a bucket brigade to move lighter items down the beach.

Life will be much simpler if you stick to a system and know exactly where every piece of equipment is carried on the rafts. Tables usually get strapped on top of dry boxes and can be used as a seat. They're more comfortable with a Paco pad on top.

On the first day of any trip there will be a lot of sorting out what gear goes in what raft, but once you have that figured out, it works best to load the rafts the same way every day.

Usually the bow and stern compartments of the raft carry things like dry bags and the groover, as well as chairs, fire pans, and other miscellaneous gear. Once everything is in place, lash it down. People sometimes choose not to rig for flipping (rigging for flipping means everything is lashed down securely, versus just throwing a net over things to hold them in place) on days when they don't anticipate any chance of losing their load. But it's a good idea to get in the habit of lashing things down every day so you are never caught off guard.

Some companies make mesh cargo bags for holding gear that fit into the bow or stern compartments of your raft. The bag has cam straps on the sides that attach to the oar frame or D rings, and hold the bag and its load suspended off the floor. You then place your cargo inside the bag, pull it together, and buckle it closed. This system is fast and, if attached properly, holds your gear in place in the event of a flip.

You can pile up a lot of gear in the bow and stern of your raft. Just don't overload your rowers, and make sure every item is strapped in and lashed down so you don't lose anything in a flip.

Another alternative is to use cargo nets to secure your loads. Cargo nets help keep things neat in your raft, and they hold gear in place in the event of a flip if the net is tied down properly. If you opt to take this route, make sure you lash down anything that is smaller than the gaps in the net so it can't float out if the raft goes upside down, and take care to tie the net down tightly so things can't slip out the sides. Some people are wary of cargo nets because they think they present an entanglement hazard. As long as the nets are tight, however, they should be fine.

Finally, in the absence of a cargo bag or net, you can lash your load into place with cam straps or webbing using a star pattern for security. Lashing gear in place is the tried-and-true method for securing your cargo. It's also the cheapest option. Make sure your cam straps pass through every single dry bag or piece of gear in the pile to ensure it's tied down. The star pattern—think of a Star of David formed by straps running between D rings on the tubes—helps keep everything in place, which is critical if your raft ends up running a rapid upside down.

To secure your load, make sure your lash straps go through the handles of your dry bags and are attached directly to the frame or D rings on the raft tubes at multiple points.

Fill the dry boxes and coolers, latch them closed, and lash them down with two straps per box.

Ammo cans, rocket boxes, and water jugs can get lashed in on either side of the cockpit, in the bow and stern compartments, or on top of the frame. Make sure you balance them out as much as possible to help keep your raft evenly weighted. Smaller items—day bags, etc.—get lashed on as is convenient.

In the absence of a frame—such as when carrying cargo in a paddle raft—use the star pattern to lash your equipment into the central cockpit between the thwarts.

This brings up the question of how to distribute the weight in your raft. It's best to try to make the raft as evenly weighted as possible, and just a little bow heavy. A raft that is too light upfront is easier to flip. You can use your passengers to help even things out or to weigh down the bow in a rapid if necessary. Side-to-side balance helps ensure your raft is maneuverable in whitewater.

For items that ride in the same place all the time, such as your dry boxes and coolers, leave the lash straps that hold them in place, secured to the frame throughout your trip, so you don't have to replace them every day.

Also, it's nice for newer rafters to have lighter rafts so they have an easier time moving their boat where they want it. For that reason let the experienced folks take the heavier loads—at least at first.

Camp check

Once the rafts are loaded, have someone take a quick wander through camp to make sure nothing has been left behind, including bits of trash. On popular rivers, camps are used almost every night during the high season, so leave yours clean for the next visitors, as well as for the animals that live in the area.

HITTING THE WATER

When everything is loaded and everyone is ready, take a few minutes to review the plan for the day. Let people look at the river map so they know what to expect before you get moving. Point out any rapids you plan to stop and scout, and decide where you want to camp or tell people where you are camping if your site has been assigned on your permit. Point out possible lunch spots and hikes. Do this early enough so people can keep their hiking gear out if they want to go for a walk. You can always revise this plan on the water—scouting

WIND

It's pretty common to get high winds whipping down river corridors. Some rivers are more notorious than others, but all of them have their moments. Make sure you don't leave things scattered around when packing and unpacking. Tents can fly away at a moment's notice if you leave them unattended. Weight light items down with a rock or ammo box. Tie your tent off to rocks, trees, or stakes. Beware of small, lightweight stakes in dry sand: If it's really windy they might not hold. Try placing piles of rocks on top of the stakes to provide added security. If you are drying your river clothes, make sure they are secured and can't blow away in the wind. Put things inside your dry bag or in a tent so you don't lose anything to the elements.

more or less than planned, for example—but it helps for everyone to have a general vision of what is in store for the day.

Once on the river designate lead and sweep boats. You can float between the two at your own pace, but if you lose sight of each other, eddy out and regroup. Make sure the sweep boat carries the wrap kit (for getting a raft unpinned) so it's upstream of a boat in need. Your teammates are your support and safety system on the river, but they need to be able to get to you to provide assistance.

MAKING CAMP

On rivers that do not have assigned campsites, chat with other groups as you pass each other on the river to figure out where they are heading. If you want to spend the night at a popular site, plan to get there early as you may find yourself out of luck at the end of a long day if you arrive and find a group is already there. Have a backup plan, just in case.

Establishing your camp is basically the opposite of taking it down. If everyone pitches in, the setup will go quickly.

Make sure you leave your rafts tied up to a tree, boulder, or sand stake so they remain secure on the beach overnight.

RAFTING WITH KIDS

Kids love raft trips, and it's a great way for families to camp together in the wilderness without the adults having to schlep heavy loads around on their backs. But there are hazards, especially with little kids who aren't really aware of danger or their own susceptibility to it. To make sure you have a fun, safe trip it's smart to establish clear guidelines both for the kids and for the adults who are coming along.

River trips are the ultimate family vacation. You're away from the distractions of daily life, unplugged from your electronics, and out in nature together—what more can you ask?

PICK THE RIGHT RIVER

The right river will be determined by the age of your kids and the experience level of your rafters. That said, if you are traveling with infants and toddlers, your best bet is to stick to rivers rated Class II or below, unless you are very confident in your boating skills or it's easy to walk the bigger rapids. The idea of a toddler or an infant swimming a Class III rapid is pretty terrifying, so you should do everything you can to prevent that from happening.

Avoid running rivers during peak flows. Low water generally means less stress, less pushy currents, less debris, and, in general, a more mellow run with your kids.

Remember, river trips with young children should only be undertaken with a highly competent crew. You don't want to be on a steep learning curve with your precious cargo.

As your kids get older, you can up the ante on your river trips, especially if they've grown up on the water. By the time they are teenagers, you can be on almost any river with them, as long as you—and they—have the requisite skills and experience to be there.

Rafting with kids is all about creating a positive, safe environment for them to be on the river. It's not the time to test your rafting skills. Pick a river that will allow you—and your kids—to relax and have fun.

SUPERVISION

Children of all ages can safely travel down a river, but when they are little, they need constant supervision. Assign someone to watch over the youngsters at all times, and make sure children are wearing their PFDs when they are playing in or near the water.

When you go through whitewater, put kids in the raft that is the least likely to encounter any trouble and hang on to them tightly.

In camp, assign one adult to kid duty so the little ones are supervised at all times. It's not a bad idea to invite along single friends, grandparents, or to have a designated nanny on your trip to spread out that role. The more extra hands on deck the better when it comes to making sure kids are well supervised and cared for on a river trip.

WATER SMARTS

Help your kids develop their water sense early. Babies can be swimming at a remarkably early age. If you plan to spend a lot of time on the river with your family, it's a good idea to start swimming lessons when your kids are infants to ensure they are comfortable in water.

Let your kids practice floating in the river in the defensive swimmer position so they are comfortable in the water.

On the river, let your kids float around in the river in their PFDs to get a feeling for what it's like to be in the water. You can get toddlers to jump off the raft and float alongside in the current in flat water sections of the river so they get a chance to practice the proper swimming position. Train them to yell loudly when they go into the water, or to blow their whistle if they have one, to alert others. Even if they're just playing around, if kids know to yell when they go into the water, they will do it instinctively in an emergency. When it's time to pull kids back on board, have them swim up to the raft so you can pull them out with their PFDs.

Kids under six or seven should wear their PFDs anytime they are near the water. Invest in a good life jacket. It should be comfortable and Coast Guard–approved. Infants and toddlers should wear PFDs that have a strap running between their legs, a padded head support that will help flip them onto their backs in the event of a swim, and a grab loop so it's easy to pull them out of the water.

Little kids should be in their PFDs whenever they are near the water. Make sure your child's life jacket is Coast Guard-approved, fits properly, comes with a padded head flap, and has a strap running between the legs to keep the vest from sliding up.

COMFORT

We've all seen kids shivering by the side of a pool or pond, their lips blue. Despite their chill, they are always ready to go back in the water at a moment's notice. Children are not great about taking care of themselves. They will go hard until they collapse. They'll ignore the heat or cold rather than forgo a chance to play with their friends. That means the adults have to ensure the little ones are dressed for the weather conditions.

Make sure you pack appropriate clothing for your kids. Don't skimp. It's more likely than not that the kids will end up soaking wet (and happy), so you'll want to always have warm, dry clothes available for them. In addition, slather kids with sunscreen and try to get them to wear a hat, a sun shirt, and sunglasses to protect them against the constant glare of the sun.

Kids aren't great at regulating their temperature, so the adults on your trip need to be on top of it, helping them cover up to avoid the sun or bundle up to avoid the cold.

FIRST AID

You should carry a well-stocked first aid kit whenever you are out on a multiday river trip, but there are a few extras worth considering with kids. First, consider allergies. You may not know if your kid is allergic to something if he or she has never been exposed, so it's a good idea to bring an antihistamine, as well as epinephrine, in case your child has an anaphylactic reaction unexpectedly. Obviously, if you know your child is sensitive, come prepared.

More likely your biggest concern will be lesser reactions to things like bee stings, wasp bites, poison ivy or oak, and mosquito bites. Carry a wash like Tecnu or Ivarest to use after contact with poison oak or ivy to help prevent a rash from developing. Anti-itch cream, calamine lotion, anti-sting sticks, and hydrocortisone creams can be helpful to keep kids comfortable if they have a reaction to bites or plants. If you anticipate lots of bugs or poison ivy, make sure to pack long-sleeved cotton shirts and long cotton pants to cover up your kids' skin while around camp.

If you are traveling in tick country, do tick checks before bed. Look in warm, dark places: behind the ears, in the groin, under the arms. To remove a tick, grasp it as close to the head as possible (tweezers help) and pull slowly and steadily upward. After the tick is out, clean the area thoroughly with soap and water. If you have had to remove an embedded tick from your child, keep an eye on the bite area and the child to watch for any reactions or illness. Most tick-borne illnesses have a slow onset, so it's unlikely anything will occur on the river, but you want to be on the lookout for problems just in case.

Finally, pack lots of Band-Aids. All parents know the magical power of a Band-Aid on an owie, so carry a stash of fun Band-Aids to cheer them up if they get a scratch.

BUILD A NEST OR SANCTUARY

Take time to build a nest on the raft for your little ones, where they can get out of the sun and take a nap. A Paco pad under an umbrella makes a comfortable crash pad for kids who need a break. Some people bring along a portable crib or playpen to set up on the beach and corral little ones in a safe place for quiet time.

Create a comfortable spot on the raft where your kids can crash out, nap, or escape the sun.

For little ones, a car seat can make a great throne for them to ride in as they float down the river.

ESSENTIALS

Everyone on your trip will have a day bag packed with his or her essentials that is readily accessible during the day. For kids this is especially important. Pack their day bags full of snacks, clean diapers, layers, rain gear, and maybe a toy or book to help keep them entertained and comfortable throughout the day.

BOUNDARIES

River trips are a great opportunity for kids to enjoy freedom, but it's key to establish some boundaries to protect them. There are all kinds of potential hazards on the river—water, wasps, bees, poison ivy, snakes, falls, rocks, etc.—so give the kids a sense of where they can be unrestricted in their play and where they need to be with a grown-up.

Chores

Children like to be part of the team, so give them chores. For little ones, these chores can be simple. They can help set up bee traps or roll out the kitchen

Kids love to be part of the team, so when the water is flat and you aren't in a hurry, let them try rowing.

floor. They can carry light things up from the raft. They can get on the oars and try rowing. They can be in charge of picking up microtrash around camp. In fact, you can make a picking up trash or smashing aluminum cans a game to add to the fun.

Older kids and teenagers can take on more challenging tasks. When my daughter was sixteen and on our latest river trip she and other teens on a river trip had their own cook group in charge of all the meals and cleanup for a day. Start out by having kids be part of your cook team so they know how things work, and then let them graduate to being on their own.

Get kids in their own boats

One way to instill a love for river life is to get kids into their own boat. You can bring along inflatable kayaks, stand-up paddleboards (SUPs), packrafts or hard-shell kayaks for them to play around in. When they are little they may need to be in the small boat with an adult, but later on they can fend for themselves.

You can always lash small boats onto your raft for rapids or when the wind starts blowing upstream, making paddling alone more miserable than fun.

Keep your days short

Kids get antsy on boats if they don't have an outlet for their energy and interests, so it's a good idea to limit your time on the river. Take breaks onshore every couple of hours to give kids a chance to run and play. Don't try to do a lot of long-mileage days. Traveling with kids should be slow and leisurely if you want them to have fun.

Fishing

Bring along fishing equipment and let kids fish off the raft as you float down-stream. Make sure you know the regulations, and talk to kids about precautions for casting around people and boats. But other than that, they can pretty much be on their own. Fishing gives kids a lot of independence, and many of them get thoroughly mesmerized by casting in the river and looking for fish.

Fishing can be a great way for kids to explore the natural world and learn a skill.

Art supplies, books, games

Pack art supplies, books, and games to help keep children entertained. You can give them some guidance—for example, ask them to draw a flower or animal that you see. Such guided discovery helps kids learn about the natural world around them.

POOPING

For kids in diapers, you'll need to bring along some kind of separate diaper pail for transporting dirty diapers. A rocket box or a 5-gallon bucket with a lid and lined with a trash compacter bag works well as a portable diaper pail. Place used baby wipes in with the dirty diapers. Some people like to let their kids run around naked in camp to help minimize the number of diapers they need. This works great if you can manage the sun exposure. Be sure to keep an eye on them so you can clean up if they have an accident on shore.

Toddlers and elementary-age kids will probably need some coaching on how to use the groover. Go with them to show them how it's done, and to make sure they are leaving it in good condition after every use—at least the first time. After they get the hang of it, you may be able to let them go on their own. You can decide if they are ready.

Kids will find all sorts of ways to have fun on a river trip, and their joy will undoubtedly add to yours.

HAVE FUN

Kids give you an excuse to play on the river. You can have water fights, jump off rocks, swim from the raft, float through easy rapids, fish off the back of the boat, build sand castles on the beach, or play organized games around camp. Be creative, spontaneous, and relaxed. Let children guide you. Their curiosity can help you see the world in a new way. Finally, kids can lighten up the mood and get everyone to chill out and find their inner child, if we let them.

Floating down rivers with your kids can be an incredibly bonding experience and will create memories that last a lifetime.
MOLLY ABSOLON

CHAPTER ELEVEN
LEAVE NO TRACE

Wilderness travel comes with responsibility. The things that make it special—untrammeled nature, wildlife, clean air and water, flowers, trees, and scenic splendor—require respect and care to protect them for future generations.

The Leave No Trace Center for Outdoor Ethics has created seven general principles that guide backcountry travelers on how to move through the wilderness without causing harm to the land, water, and wildlife. These principles are meant to be guidelines that can be adapted to different circumstances and environments. They are not hard and fast rules, but suggestions that allow you to travel lightly on the land that you love.

Thousands of people travel along popular river corridors every year. To help keep these special places special, all of us need to work to minimize our impact by following the Leave No Trace principles.

Many permitted rivers have additional requirements to help minimize impacts along the river corridor. These regulations make a lot of sense when you think about the fact that hundreds, if not thousands, of boaters are using the same campsites over and over again every year. Without special care, those sites would soon be trashed and unusable.

The basic seven principles are:

1. **Plan ahead and prepare.** Know the regulations and special concerns for the area you'll visit. Prepare for extreme weather, hazards, and emergencies by carrying the proper gear and obtaining the required skills so you aren't forced to compromise your LNT ethics to ensure your safety. Visit in small groups when possible. Repackage food and plan meals carefully to minimize waste.

2. **Travel and camp on durable surfaces.** Durable surfaces include established trails and campsites, rock, gravel, dry grasses, snow, and rivers. Along most river corridors the lowest impact sites are established campsites on beaches or gravel bars along the water's edge. Good campsites are found, not made. Altering a site is not necessary. In popular areas, concentrate

Make sure your group knows the rules and regulations for the river you will be descending before you hit the water.

use on existing campsites, walk single file in the middle of trails, keep campsites small, and focus activity in areas where vegetation is absent. In pristine areas, disperse use to prevent the creation of campsites and trails, move camp frequently, and avoid places where impacts are just beginning.

3. **Dispose of waste properly.** Pack it in, pack it out. Inspect your campsite and rest areas for trash or spilled foods. Pack out all trash, leftover food, and litter. Food scraps attract animals to campsites. Along river corridors where sites are heavily used, this creates problem animals, so keep a clean camp.

On popular rivers most campsites are sacrificial sites—that is, they've been used over and over again and show obvious signs of human traffic. But camping on beaches helps keep the impact down and keeps the area in good shape for the next visitors.

Disposing of waste properly includes depositing human waste appropriately. In most river corridors this means packing the poop out, usually in a groover of some kind. It's a good idea to have some kind of portable sanitation system, such as human waste bags, for an emergency when the groover is on the raft and unavailable.

Dishwashing and bathing regulations are different on different rivers. Sometimes you do everything in the river; other times you wash above the high-water mark. Make sure to read the regulations for the river you are visiting to ensure you abide by the rules.

For urination, as with wastewater, regulations vary, but usually they require travelers to urinate directly into the river. There are some areas where this practice is frowned upon so check with land managers before your trip to determine the preferred practice.

4. **Leave what you find.** Preserve the past. Examine but do not touch cultural or historic structures and artifacts. Leave plants, rocks, and other natural objects as you find them.

It's not uncommon to find potsherds around cultural sites. If they have already been collected and moved to one area, go ahead and leave them in place. If you find a piece on its own, don't move it. It's nice to find things in a more natural setting.
STEFANIE VANDAELE

Avoid introducing or transporting nonnative species. This is particularly important with boats. Boats are known to spread invasives like zebra mussels. Make sure you clean and dry your boating gear carefully after every trip to help reduce the chance you are inadvertently carrying a hitchhiker.

Do not build structures, furniture, or dig trenches.

5. **Minimize campfire impacts.** Campfires can cause lasting impacts to the backcountry if they are used improperly. Use fires with care and only in areas where they are allowed and wood is plentiful.

On most permitted rivers, users are required to carry a fire pan for their campfires and to pack out all ashes. Some rivers also require you to carry all your firewood. Away from regulated rivers, build fires in established fire rings, fire pans, or on mineral soil on a beach or gravel bar.

Burn all wood and coals to ash and put out campfires completely. On regulated rivers, place the cold ash in a rocket box to be disposed of when you get off the river. On unregulated wilderness rivers, spread cold ashes away from the river. Make sure the fire is totally out to avoid accidentally starting a wildfire.

6. **Respect wildlife.** Observe wildlife from a distance. Do not follow or approach wild animals. Be aware of the fact that you travel quickly and quietly in a raft and can often come upon animals unexpectedly. Try to make noise to warn them of your approach. If you are causing animals distress, either pull over and let them get away from you, or move on downriver and away. Avoid wildlife during sensitive times, such as mating or nesting season, in spring when animals are raising young, or in winter when conditions are harsh.

Never feed animals. Feeding animals damages their health, alters natural behaviors, and exposes them to predators and other dangers. Feeding includes leaving food scraps around camp. Be sure to keep your camp clean to avoid creating camp robbers.

Control your pets at all times, or leave them at home.

7. **Be considerate of other visitors.** Respect other visitors and protect the quality of their experience. Be courteous. Yield to other users on the trail or on the river. Take breaks away other visitors. Let nature's sounds prevail.

When floating on rivers, don't pull in to a beach where another party is taking a break or camping unless you have no choice or are visiting a

On regulated rivers you are often required to pack out the ashes from your fires. Make sure they are cold before you load them up.

It's common to see bighorn sheep, deer, moose, waterfowl, and other wildlife as you float downriver. Try not to disturb them as you pass. If you see signs of agitation, move away and leave them alone.

special site. Some rivers have assigned campsites; on others the campsites are first come, first served. If you know you want to stop at a specific spot for the night, get moving early in the day to ensure you get there before someone else does.

SPECIAL CONSIDERATIONS FOR RAFTING IN BEAR COUNTRY

Some of the best rafting in the world takes place in bear country, so it's important to know how to camp and travel to protect yourself and the bears.

Most bears don't want anything to do with people. But if you stumble upon one in the midst of a meal, protecting its young, or simply by surprise, the bear's natural reaction is to protect itself, its food, and its young. Rarely, you may encounter an aberrant bear that is aggressive for no clear reason. In either case, one too many encounters between bears and humans, and game managers end up "removing" the bear—a euphemism for killing it. To avoid this, we need to be thoughtful when we travel in bear country.

The number one strategy for avoiding an unexpected encounter with a bear is to make noise. Travel in groups when you hike away from camp—and by groups, we mean three or more people close together. If you get spread out, the impact of your group is lost.

If you know you will be traveling in bear country, make sure you take special precautions to protect yourself, your food, and the bears.

Carry bear spray. Bear spray has been proven the most effective way to stop a bear attack. But you need to have your spray handy. Having the spray in the top of your pack or in a dry bag on your raft does you no good whatsoever if a bear starts to charge you. If you plan to hike away from the river in bear country, several members of your party should carry bear spray. Make sure they have practiced shooting it off quickly so that if they find themselves in a situation where they need it, they'll be able to suppress their natural urge to run and respond appropriately.

The recommended behavior in a bear encounter is for everyone to group up so you look big. Talk quietly so the bear gets a sense of what you are. Pull your bear spray out. If the bear charges, you want to deploy the bear spray when the animal is roughly 25 to 30 feet away. Be aware of the wind direction. If the wind is coming toward you, wait longer. You may need to spray multiple times to deter a bear.

If bear spray does not cause the bear to turn and run, drop to the ground and play dead, curling up under your backpack if you are wearing one, and protecting your neck and head with your hands. In many cases, the bears will lose interest if they no longer perceive you to be a threat. If a bear seems to be trying to eat you, fight aggressively.

Needless to say, playing dead, holding your ground—even getting your bear spray out of its holster and administering a blast—take a lot of composure in the face of a charging bear, especially when your instincts are screaming "run." For all these reasons it's important to do everything you can to avoid bear encounters and to practice the appropriate response so it's instinctive when you get surprised.

Remember to store all food in dry boxes or coolers on the raft to keep bears out. Keep all your smelly stuff stored with your food. That includes toothpaste, sunscreen, and bug repellant—anything that doesn't smell like nature. Sleep away from the kitchen area.

FINAL THOUGHTS ON LNT

If you've traveled down any popular, permit-controlled river, you know that there are hundreds, if not thousands, of people using the same campsites throughout the rafting season, and yet most of these sites are remarkably clean. That's because of LNT. River regulations are designed to minimize camper impacts, and if we all follow the rules and do our part to clean up after ourselves, the river will remain wild and beautiful despite our numbers.

Take time to ensure you have the equipment you need to travel safely. When emergencies or shortages occur, LNT tends to fly out the window. That makes sense—after all, personal safety is our No. 1 priority—but it's a shame to sacrifice the river corridor because we neglected to bring enough fuel and have to build a big fire to stay warm.

If we do our part to take care of the river, it will continue to be healthy, beautiful, and enjoyable for all of us.

CHAPTER TWELVE

RIVER-SPECIFIC HEALTH AND FIRST AID

If you plan to spend a lot of time on wilderness rivers, you should take a wilderness first aid course and CPR. Wilderness first aid is different from the basics you learn in the city, where an ambulance is usually just a few minutes away. On a river trip, it can take hours, if not days, for you to get help, so you need to know how to stabilize and care for an injured or sick person for a long time.

This book is not a first aid guide. However, there are some river-specific health and safety concerns that are worth mentioning.

COLD-WATER SWIM

Most of the time, an unexpected flip and swim are relatively inconsequential. Sure, it can be startling and even scary, but it's usually not hard to get back into your raft. Flipping your raft happens when you push your boating skills and tackle more difficult objectives. It's one way that you get better, and if you are wearing the right clothes for a swim, you'll be fine. Don't panic if you come out of your raft and end up in the water.

As mentioned earlier, you should assume the defensive swimmer position—on your back; feet up and pointing downstream—unless you decide to actively swim to avoid a hazard or reach safety, in which case you'll be on your belly swimming freestyle. Whichever position you are in, keep your feet up! Breathe in the troughs between waves to avoid a mouthful of water, and try to relax. Unless you are in an extreme situation, you will be fine. Obviously bad stuff happens on rivers, but most of the time swimming a rapid is more uncomfortable than dangerous.

Going for a swim is not a health emergency, but it can become one if the water is cold and the swimmer isn't dressed for the conditions.

That said, you don't want to underestimate the dangers of swimming in cold-water rapids. Swimmers can get chilled and exhausted quickly if they are in cold water for a long time. Remember, the rule of thumb for unprotected cold-water immersion is 1–10–1: 1 minute of cold water shock, when your breathing and heart rate accelerate; 10 minutes of functional movement, when you have the physical power and strength to fight to help yourself; 1 hour before you pass out from hypothermia if you remain submerged. Obviously, these times are drawn out if you are wearing proper attire, such as a dry suit. But it's still important to recognize that people can get cold fast, and may be unable to help themselves.

If a member of your party swims, your first step is to get him or her out of the water. However, it's important to remember that in all first aid and rescue situations, the well-being of the rescuer is the No. 1 priority. Don't jeopardize your safety or the safety of other members of your party to perform a rescue. If you cannot help someone without risking your own life, you should not attempt to help. That sounds cold-hearted, but the reality is things can escalate quickly and casualties mount when people attempt to be superheroes. Don't take unnecessary risks. Do what you can but make sure you stay safe.

HOW TO PULL A SWIMMER ONTO A RAFT

1. Grab the swimmer by the shoulder straps of his PFD.
2. Consider pushing down on him first to gain some extra bounce as his PFD pops up due to its buoyancy.
3. Fall backward into the raft, pulling the swimmer in with you. Use your weight and gravity, not your strength, to pull him in.

Help swimmers get back into the raft by pulling them up with their life jackets. Swimmers can make things easier by pulling up on the grab line and kicking their legs aggressively while still in the water.

Once you've pulled a swimmer out of the water, his or her condition determines your next step. Most of the time the person will be just fine. But you do need to be prepared to administer first aid if the swimmer is cold or injured.

Do a quick patient assessment to determine the swimmer's condition. This includes the ABCDEs of first aid (airway, breathing, circulation, disability, and environment). If your patient's ABCs are compromised—he or she isn't breathing or is bleeding profusely, for example—you need to stop and treat that problem right away. These are life-threatening problems, and your patient will die if you don't address them as quickly as possible.

THREATS TO LIFE: THE ABCDEs

There are a few simple things you can do in the first five minutes after an accident to save someone's life. They include the following:

- **Airway:** People die if they do not have an airway, or an open passage to get oxygen into their lungs. If someone is drowning, get him to shore and immediately check to see if his airway is open. If your patient can talk, he has an airway, is breathing, and has a pulse. That means you can move on to see if he is bleeding or has suffered some traumatic injury. If your patient is unconscious and you cannot detect breathing, tilt his head back and lift his chin. If you think there could be a spinal cord injury, just lift his chin without tilting his head. Often this will be enough to restore breathing.

- **Breathing:** Look, listen, and feel for signs of breathing. Is your patient's chest rising? Can you feel air against your cheek? Can you hear breathing sounds? If you do not detect any signs of breathing after twenty seconds or so, maintain your patient's head tilt and chin lift, and blow two quick breaths into her mouth. If the breaths go in, continue rescue breathing at a rate of about twenty breaths per minute. If the breaths do not go in, reposition the head and try again. If you still cannot get air in, look in the person's mouth to see if there is anything obstructing the airway. If so remove it; if not, reposition her head with the head-tilt, chin-lift technique and try again to blow air into the lungs. Keep trying until you succeed or someone with more experience and training takes over.

  Drowning—or near-drowning—victims will often throw up. Anticipate this and be prepared to roll them on their side so they do not aspirate. If you have a face mask, use it to protect yourself from vomit while performing rescue breathing. If not, you may want to place a bandanna over the victim's mouth to serve as a physical barrier.

- **Circulation:** If you are trained in CPR, once you establish breathing—either because the patient is breathing on her own or you are doing rescue breathing—check for a pulse and go into the CPR routine. If you are not trained, continue rescue breathing as necessary and check for bleeding by sweeping your hands all over your patient's body to look for blood. Remember, if your patient is wearing a dry suit or rain gear, you will need to get inside his clothes to detect bleeding, as the blood will not pass through the waterproof material. If you find major hemorrhaging, try to control the bleeding by placing a sterile dressing—or whatever you have that can absorb the blood—directly onto the wound and pressing down. Elevate the area above the heart if possible.

- **Disability:** Check quickly for any obvious signs of trauma. Consider the mechanism of injury. If your patient has taken a big swim through a rocky rapid, have him lie quietly and keep his head or neck still until you can ensure he has not sustained a head or neck injury. You can immobilize your patient by having someone place a hand on his head or by placing bags around it to help remind him not to move.

- **Environment:** Remember, it's likely your patient is going to be cold. Get her out of the water and into a warm, dry place. Have her lie on a pad or something to insulate her from the ground. Replace wet clothes with dry ones and pull out a sleeping bag to help hasten the rewarming process.

  Stabilize your patient as best you can and seek help.

PATIENT EXAM

Once you've gone over the ABCs, you may want to conduct a head-to-toe exam. If your patient bumped through rocks at high speed, the mechanism for injury is real and you want to be sure he or she has no other problems, such as a head or neck injury or a broken bone. If you know the patient was just in the water for a long time and has gotten cold, you can skip this step.

Take a few minutes to ask the patient a few basic questions. You can get a good sense of a person's level of consciousness by asking his name, where he is, what day and time it is, and what happened. If your patient has trouble answering these questions, be on the lookout for further deterioration and consider the possibility of a head injury.

Any threat to life is serious. If you are deep in the wilderness, it can take a long time to get your patient to a hospital, especially if she cannot walk or boat. Monitor the individual's vital signs (pulse, respiration rate, level of consciousness, skin color and temperature, and pupil size and evenness) every half an hour or so (more if you suspect a serious injury) to keep track of her condition. A normal adult has a resting pulse between 60 and 100 beats per minute (athletes may have rates in the 40s), breathes 12 to 20 times per minute, has pink, warm, dry skin (in dark-skinned people, look at nail beds to detect this skin color), and pupils that are even in size and reactive to light. A normal level of responsiveness is demonstrated by a person who knows her name, location, the time of day, and what happened. Any signs of deterioration in these vital signs ups the urgency of the evacuation.

People often have drastically different baselines in terms of their heart rates, breathing rates, etc., so stay calm if you initially get what seem to be bad numbers for your patient's vital signs. That might be normal for them. Watch for the trend over time and if vital signs continue to worsen despite your best care, then you probably need to get your patient to advanced medical care as quickly as possible.

It is helpful to carry pain medication with you on wilderness expeditions. Recent research indicates that a maximum recommended dosage of ibuprofen taken in conjunction with the maximum recommended dosage of acetamino-phen can provide as much pain relief as prescription pain medications. You can take the ibuprofen and acetaminophen together or, better yet, stagger the two every four hours.

GETTING HELP

On remote rivers you should carry some kind of communication device that will allow you to get help in the event of an emergency. Remember, calling 911 usually isn't the best option. Check with the land managers in charge of the river you are running to find out who you should call if something goes wrong. It could be they want you to call them, or perhaps the local search and rescue group. Write down important phone numbers and store them with your communication device so they are easy to find.

SIGNS AND SYMPTOMS OF HYPOTHERMIA

Hypothermia—or too little heat—causes a gradual deterioration in a patient's mental and physical abilities. At the far end of the spectrum, when patients are severely hypothermic, they are unresponsive. Severe hypothermia is deadly, so it's important to recognize what's happening and take action to stop it immediately. Your patient doesn't have to take a swim to be hypothermic, and neither do you. Hypothermia can happen when boating in cold wet conditions, so be prepared.

As your core temperature drops, you begin to get clumsy. At first just your fine motor skills may be compromised. Your fingers don't work, and you can't zip up your life jacket, for instance. If you get colder your gross motor skills begin to be affected, and you may find yourself stumbling when you try to walk. Often hypothermic patients become apathetic or grumpy. Speech may be altered. As you slide from mild into moderate hypothermia, your level of consciousness deteriorates and you may answer questions inappropriately or be confused. Concisely put, the patient has the "umbles": They fumble, stumble, mumble, and grumble.

It can be easier to detect signs of hypothermia in someone other than yourself. Keep an eye on each other when you are paddling in wet, cold conditions. Boaters say 50 degrees and rainy is prime hypothermia weather if you are unprepared, so pay attention if you are out in those conditions. And pay attention to swimmers; they will get cold much faster.

Our bodies lose heat in a number of ways, one of which is convection, or the loss of heat to water or air moving past our skin. The rate of convective heat loss depends on the difference in temperature between your body and the water, which means it can be as much as 25 times as chilling as standing in still, warm air if conditions are extreme. Remember this when you launch on a glacial river.

Treatment for mild to moderate hypothermia

It is pretty easy to warm up when you first detect signs that you are getting too cold. Get out of the offending environment. Change into dry clothes or seek shelter. Do some jumping jacks, run around, or swing your arms and legs. Exercise ups our heat generation by 15 to 18 times. If you feel chilled, moving will help warm you up.

As you get colder, you'll grow more apathetic and may just feel like curling up in a ball. Exercise can still help, but most likely you'll need someone to force you to move. As a caregiver, you may have to be more assertive in your treatment if your patient is becoming lethargic. Again, make sure the patient is in warm, dry clothes and out of the offending elements. Pull out your stove and heat up some water for a hot beverage if the individual is able to drink from a cup without assistance.

You may want to light a fire. Some people carry an emergency reflective blanket in their first aid kits for hypothermia treatment. If you have a fire, your patient can sit in front of it wearing the emergency blanket like a cape to trap the fire's radiant heat.

If your patient is not responding to these treatments, it's time to get more aggressive. If you are on a river trip you'll have camping gear along, so you can make a hypothermic wrap to warm your patient. To make a wrap, place a ground cloth or a tent fly on the ground. Lay a sleeping pad in the middle of the tarp kitty-corner to the midline. Place a sleeping bag on top of the pad. Have your patient strip down to a dry base layer, put on a warm hat, and get into the sleeping bag. You will probably need to provide assistance.

Meanwhile, heat up a couple of liters of water on a stove or fire. The water does not have to boil. You just want it to be hot enough to warm—not burn—your patient. Pour the water into two or three water bottles. If it feels too hot to be next to your skin, wrap the bottle in a sock or T-shirt.

Place the water bottles in the bag with your patient. It's nice to have the bottles near the patient's core: between the legs in the groin area or under the armpits. Zip up the sleeping bag and snug it tightly around your patient's head, leaving the face clear. Next fold the corner of the tarp by the patient's feet in over the sleeping bag, and then bring the sides of the tarp across him or her, tucking them in tightly. Wrap the tarp around the patient's head. Don't cover the face. Your patient will be swaddled in the tarp and should look like a burrito when you are done.

Our bodies warm slowly. If we get really cold, it could take hours for us to rewarm. During that time, you'll need to replace the hot water bottles periodically. People who are less cold will recover more rapidly. Moderately hypothermic people are wiped out by the experience. If your patient takes hours to rewarm, he or she may take days to feel normal. In this scenario, you should not expect the individual to be able to row or paddle effectively.

If your patient is severely hypothermic, gently wrap him or her up in a hypothermic wrap. Do not be too jarring or rough in your handling, as sudden movements can cause heart problems in a severely cold human. Place hot water bottles in with the patient but be extra careful the bottles are not too hot. These patients will be unable to tell you if they are getting burned. The hypothermic wrap will not rewarm this person, but it can help prevent further heat loss. Go for help. This individual needs medical attention, but even if he or she appears dead, there is hope. Some severely hypothermic people are successfully rewarmed.

Ultimately, hypothermia is preventable if you pay attention to the environmental conditions, carry the appropriate gear, and respond quickly when you see the signs and symptoms of someone getting too cold. Aim to stop the problem when you can still do jumping jacks to get warm.

DROWNING

Drowning or near drowning causes complex physiological responses. As a first responder, the details of what is going on are less important than the steps you can take to help save your patient.

One of the first things to be aware of is that drowning people do not always present in the thrashing, yelling, splashing way we expect (because we've watched too many movies). People who are drowning are often exhausted and can barely stay above the water. All their energy goes into trying to get a breath. They don't have time to yell for help. For this reason, it's important to keep your eyes on your partners if they go for a swim, and to try to get to them as quickly as possible.

This passivity changes if you get in the water next to someone who is drowning. Victims often panic and try to climb on top of rescuers in an attempt to get to the surface and air. You are better off approaching a drowning person with some kind of flotation device or a throw rope than with your own body. Sometimes that is impossible, and advanced swiftwater rescue courses will teach you how to dive in and swim to the assistance of victims. But this technique is not without risks, and rescuers are usually connected to shore with a rope to help pull them back to safety. If you are planning to boat highly technical rivers, gaining this skill is imperative. If you are in more moderate water, you are better off focusing on using a throw rope or your boat to assist a swimmer.

If you pull an unresponsive victim out of the river, go immediately to your ABCs. CPR and rescue breathing can be effective in near-drowning situations. Be prepared for your patient to vomit up ingested water. Call for help.

Flush drowning

Flush drowning occurs when a victim is denied air by rough water or from being held underwater by the force of the current. Flush drownings typically occur during high water, when rivers are in flood stage, or in long stretches of continuous rapids where it's difficult for swimmers to escape the current or rescuers to come to their assistance.

OTHER RIVER AILMENTS

Trench foot

Trench—or immersion—foot is nerve damage caused by prolonged exposure to cold, wet conditions. Trench foot is a nonfreezing injury and is most common in places like the Arctic, or occurs during early season travel when temperatures are cool and the weather wet.

Trench foot can be extremely painful and most sufferers cannot walk. Treatment is rest and pain medication, but it's unlikely that the kind of pain meds most of us carry in our first aid kits will touch the pain the victim will experience. Only heavy-duty meds can dull the pain of acute immersion foot, so most people need to be evacuated.

Avoiding immersion foot is the best medicine. To avoid trench foot make sure you do not tolerate cold feet. Wearing neoprene socks, GORE-TEX socks, or booties on the river can help. Dry suits with built-in socks are even better because your feet will not be wet during the day. If you feel your feet getting numb, stop and warm them up. Change your socks. Warm your feet on someone's belly. Swing your legs. Get out of your boat and run around. Consider wearing knee-high rubber boots or even waders to keep your feet dry, but remember these things can drag you down if they fill up with water so aren't recommended on rivers where you might take an unplanned swim.

Hand and foot cracks

If your hands and feet are wet all the time, you may end up with painful cracks in your skin. To help prevent cracking, wear socks and gloves, especially when you sleep at night. Slather your hands with a thick cream: Bag Balm, Vaseline, or Eucerin all work well to help keep your feet moist.

If you develop painful cracks, you can seal them closed with Super Glue or Nu Skin. Super Glue tubes dry out quickly in hot weather, so instead of bringing one tube, throw a handful of single-use containers in your first aid kit in case you end up with cracks.

It's also not uncommon to develop raw spots where the grit from silty water gets into your shoes and rubs away the skin. You can help prevent rubbing by wearing socks—even with sandals—and making sure your feet are dry and clean at night when you are sitting around camp.

Sunburn, sun bumps, and cold sores

Being out on the water intensifies the power of the sun, making you more susceptible to burns. Intense UV exposure also can cause sun bumps, or an itchy rash on the back of your hands and cheeks, and may trigger the development of cold sores on your lips. As a boater, you want to be aware of these possibilities, and take precautions to wear adequate sunscreen, as well as sun hats and maybe even gloves to protect your skin. (Lightweight gardening gloves work well in hot weather; neoprene gloves are best when it's cold.)

Poison ivy and poison oak

Poison ivy and poison oak are common along many river corridors. Learn to identify them so you can avoid an encounter. To help remember what these plants look like, remember "Leaves of three, let it be," as both poison oak and poison ivy have leaves clumped in groups of three.

If you are sensitive to poison ivy or poison oak, bring along something like Tecnu or Ivarest to wash your skin in case you accidentally come into contact with the plant. This may prevent you from developing a rash. It's also a good idea to pack calamine lotion or anti-itch cream, like hydrocortisone, to help deal with the discomfort of a poison oak or ivy rash.

Poison ivy and poison oak can be beautiful when they turn red in the fall, but they can also make your trip miserable if your skin comes in contact with them. Know what poison ivy and poison oak look like so you can avoid them.

Bees and wasps

Unfortunately, it's common in many river camps to be surrounded by yellow jackets or bees. Bring along a few traps to put up in camp to help keep them out of the kitchen. Wasps seem to be attracted to meat, so you can put meat in the traps to improve their efficacy. If you or any members of your party get stung, it's nice to have some kind of sting relief medication in your first aid kit. And it goes without saying that people with bee allergies should carry an antihistamine and some form of epinephrine in case they get stung.

PERSONAL HYGIENE

You can get a little funky sitting in a wet boat if you do it day in and day out. And wearing a wet suit or clammy dry suit, or going without a shower for days on end, can make it hard to stay fresh as a daisy. It's important to take care of your nether parts when you are in the backcountry, and the best way to do that is by keeping clean. Lots of boaters carry a bandanna or washcloth dedicated to sponge baths, and they will clean off every day to ensure they don't end up with something itchy or painful.

Where you take your sponge bath depends on river regulations. Some say bathe in the river; others say do it 200 feet above the high-water mark. Make sure you know where you are supposed to be before you bathe. If you use soap, rinse thoroughly as soap can irritate your skin if you don't get it off. Let yourself dry completely. The key is to not let things get too damp and warm down there. That's when you run into trouble.

Just in case, throw some kind of antifungal cream, such as Monistat for yeast infections, into your first aid kit. For long trips, see if your doctor will prescribe a round of antibiotics to treat anyone who develops a bladder infection.

FURTHER EDUCATION

Wilderness trips take you far from emergency care. You are on your own out there. That solitude is what makes expeditioning exciting—but don't be reckless in your adventuring. There's a difference between a skilled backcountry traveler attempting difficult challenges and a novice getting in over his or her head. Be realistic about your skills and experience, and choose objectives conservatively. You are responsible for the health and safety of yourself and your teammates. If you plan to partake in a wilderness rafting trip, you should consider taking first aid, CPR, and a swiftwater rescue course before you go. These courses give you the tools you need to handle emergencies, improvise treatment, and get yourself out of trouble.

See the appendix for a first aid and drug kit checklist.

CHAPTER THIRTEEN
BASIC RIVER RESCUE

SAFETY TALK

It's important—even when you are out with friends—to begin the trip with some kind of safety talk to ensure that everyone in your group is on the same page. This talk can feel contrived if you've been on lots of rivers together, but it's important to check in with each other every time you head out together to make sure you have all the proper gear, you know who's in charge, and you're aware of the hazards you may meet on the river. If you are familiar with each other, the check-in can be brief. If it's your first time on a river trip with a particular group, be more thorough and take your time.

Here's a basic outline of the key points to cover:

1. Equipment check
    a. Make sure everyone has PFDs, helmets, proper boating attire, and basic safety equipment. Take time to check the fit and quality of life jackets and helmets with beginners and kids.
    b. Make sure you have first aid kits, pin kits, throw bags, repair kits, and other safety equipment, and let everyone know where these items are stored so they can be accessed quickly.
    c. Make sure you have communication devices, or have left a travel plan with others in case something happens and you don't return on time.
2. Review what to do if someone falls out of the raft or a raft flips.
3. Review commands and signals.
4. Discuss plans for group management on the river (boat order, group leader, etc.)
5. Go over the basic itinerary for the day and discuss potential hazards, rapids, the lunch stop, the campsite, day hikes, etc.

6. Discuss who will be in charge in an emergency. Share medical information as necessary.

WHEN THINGS GO WRONG

You can run into all kinds of glitches during a day on the river. Most of the time they won't be a big deal: Someone falls out of the raft and needs to be pulled out of the river, or your raft gets stuck on a rock. For minor issues you usually can respond with simple solutions that don't require equipment or skill. Remember the adage: "Go slow to go fast." Once something goes wrong you usually have time to come up with a plan. Rushing into a rescue blindly almost always causes more chaos, so pause, look around, and figure out what to do next.

You will probably find yourself on a rock or upside down at some point in your rafting career, so it's a good idea to know a little bit about basic rescue to get yourself out of trouble.

RESCUE PRIORITIES

As with first aid, your first priority in an emergency situation is your own well-being. After that you should consider the well-being of your teammates and, only when you are confident that everyone is safe, do you consider the plight of your victim. Size up the scene. This shouldn't take long, but give your-

People always come first in an emergency, followed by equipment. If you can't retrieve your raft or rafts without jeopardizing the safety of the team, leave them.

self a good fifteen to twenty seconds to look around, get a visual on everyone in your party, and figure out what is going on. This pause also allows you to calm down so you are better able to perform methodically and efficiently.

People always come first in an emergency, followed by equipment—which could be vital if you are on a multiday trip in the wilderness—and finally the environment. In a life or death situation, if you have to cut down trees to rescue someone, do it. But the hope is that you never find yourself in that situation.

Keep it simple

You are less likely to make mistakes and more likely to be successful if you keep your rescue operation as simple as possible.

In general, when rescuing a swimmer, think: **Reach, Row, Throw, or Go.** Your first thought should be: *Can **I** reach the swimmer with a paddle or my hand?*

The simplest, safest rescue is a self-rescue. If you can get yourself back into your raft on your own, do it.

If you are using a paddle, pass the T-grip to the swimmer so she has something easy to grab on to. Remember, whether you are reaching with your hand or your paddle, you need to be in a secure position so the victim won't pull you off balance and into the water.

If you are in your raft, and the line downstream is clear, **row** over to the swimmer. When you are close enough, reach out to the swimmer with your hand or paddle to pull her close to the boat. Then help her back on the raft.

When pulling someone onto the raft, grab her by the shoulder straps of her PFD. Have the swimmer kick her legs up to the surface of the water and keep kicking to help give you some momentum. Pull up and back on the PFD. Your best bet is to just fall back into the boat with the swimmer. This takes the least amount of physical strength.

If you cannot row to the swimmer, or if you are on shore, your next option is to **throw** a throw bag to her. Ropes in water can be very dangerous. In fact, the main reason rafters carry knives on their PFDs is to cut their way out of a rope that has entangled them or someone else.

Because of the risk of entanglement, you should rarely, if ever, toss a throw bag from a moving raft. Rather, throw from onshore or from a raft that is tied to shore or secure in an eddy.

In some situations, your only option is to swim, or "**go**," to your victim. However, this option exposes you to considerable danger and only should be attempted if you are trained in swiftwater rescue and have the proper equipment, such as a rescue vest, to tow your victim.

Throw ropes from shore

Often the best way to reach a swimmer is with a rope thrown from shore. It's tricky to master this skill. Throw bags don't feel or act the way a ball does when

Tossing a rope to a swimmer with accuracy can be challenging in the heat of the moment, so take time to practice using your throw bag onshore, where you can fine-tune your skills.

you throw it; you also have the current to contend with in terms of aim, and you often have only one shot to reach the victim before he or she is carried away downstream. Take time to practice tossing your throw bag to develop your accuracy and range.

Rescuer

In the best-case scenario, you have spotters posted along the sides of a rapid armed with throw bags and ready to be of assistance if someone takes a swim. Choose your location carefully. You need to be in a secure, balanced position where you can brace yourself against the weight of the swimmer. Find a spot with slow water or an eddy downstream that will serve as a safe landing zone for your victim.

If you are not already in position when your partner flips, you'll just have to run to a good spot to make a toss.

When you get in position, yell or blow your whistle to alert the swimmer to your presence and the fact that you are there to throw a rope to him or her if needed. If you can't get the swimmer's attention, don't throw the rope.

Try to throw the bag when the swimmer is straight across from you or slightly upstream, so you create an angle when the person weights the rope that will allow him or her to pendulum in to shore.

Get into an athletic stance, with your front foot braced. You may also choose to sit down after you throw the bag so you are in a stronger position to withstand the force of the swimmer and the current.

You can throw the bag overhand, underhand, or sidearm. All work. In general, overhand and sidearm throws have more distance. Underhand throws tend to be more accurate and are good for short, quick tosses. Place the bag in your throwing hand and hold the end of the rope in the other hand. Pull out a couple of arm lengths of rope before you toss so you have room to wind up for a big throw. Aim to hit the swimmer in the head with the bag. Remember to keep hold of the end of the rope so you don't throw the whole thing in the river, and remove any carabiners you may have used to clip the throw bag to your raft so you don't hit your swimmer with something hard.

When the swimmer grabs the rope, try to pull out any slack in the system and brace yourself for the impact of his or her weight. If the force feels too powerful, sit down or walk down along the shoreline to reduce the pressure on the rope. If you are having a hard time holding on, the swimmer probably is too. You can flip the rope behind your back and hip belay the victim to shore, using friction

Once the throw rope is deployed, brace yourself for the impact of the swimmer's weight. If you have more than one person on shore, they can help hold you in place, or you can brace yourself against a rock. Hold the rope around your back for added friction.
MOE WITSCHARD

from the rope running across your body to help resist the force of the river. You can also get your teammates to grab onto your PFD to help hold you in place.

Don't wrap the rope around your hands or arms for better purchase. Remember, the rope can quickly change from an aid to a deadly trap if you get entangled in it and pulled into the river.

Swimmer

If you find yourself swimming, be alert and on the lookout for a rescuer as you get carried downstream. When a throw rope lands, try as hard as you can to get to it. Grab the rope—not the bag, as there may be more line in the bag—with both hands, flip over onto your back, place the rope over the shoulder that is opposite your rescuer, and hang on tight. You'll feel a strong jerk when the slack goes out of the system and the rope goes taut. Be ready for that pull. Kick hard to help your rescuers pull you in. You will pendulum over to the shore. Don't let go or try to stand up until you are in shallow, slow-moving water.

SWIMMER RESCUES

If you must send someone out to a victim or raft, there are several techniques that you can use. Remember, the rescuer will be attached to a rope in moving water, which is dangerous. Make sure the rope is connected with a quick release mechanism so the rescuer can get out of it quickly if things go wrong.

1. **Team wade**: Rescuers can work together to wade out to someone to provide assistance. Use a big stick for support, and have team members hang onto the lead person's PFD to keep his feet down.

Two people working together are able to wade to a victim through deeper, swifter water than one person working alone.
MOE WITSCHARD

2. **Direct lower**: If you can reach a point directly upstream of the accident site, a rescuer can be lowered down to the area.
3. **Tethered swimmer**: In this situation, the rescuer is attached to a rope that is managed from the shore while he or she swims to the accident site. This technique takes skill and experience.
4. **Fixed rope**: A fixed line is a tight line across the river at water level that allows a rescuer to travel hand-over-hand along the rope to the accident site. The fixed line is tightened with a Z-drag.
5. **Zip line**: A zip line is also a tight, fixed line at water level, but it is placed at an angle to the current so the rescuer can use the current to carry him or her to the accident site.

Swimmers should place the throw rope over their outside or upstream shoulders and flip over onto their backs, kicking hard to help the rescuers. This swimmer will pivot downstream and into shore as the rope gets taut.
MOE WITSCHARD

SWIMMING REVISITED

We've already talked about defensive and aggressive swimming in a rapid, but there are a few more things to consider. One is that you can use all the techniques you use in your raft with your body. You can swim for an eddy if you want to get out of the current. You can angle your body and ferry. The key is to keep your feet up at all times to avoid any chance of foot entrapment.

If you go over a big drop or into a hole, curl up. The turbulence of the drop or hole can toss you around, so keeping your arms and legs pulled in close helps reduce the likelihood of entrapment or injury. Once you are on the surface, reorient yourself and figure out what comes next. Some hydraulics are difficult to escape. You can try to get to the side or downstream edge of the hydraulic and reach your arm or paddle out over the boil line into the main current, which may pull you out. If this doesn't work, you may need to go deep. Dive down to the bottom where the water is usually moving downstream and see if you can ride that current out. This all sounds very scary—and if you've ever been in a recirculating hole you would probably agree that it is, in fact, very scary—but these kinds of holes are not that common on Class III rivers at moderate flows. Still, it helps to have an understanding of what is happening so in the event you find yourself being tossed around, you can be proactive in your efforts to get out.

GETTING BACK ON YOUR RAFT

The best place to be if you come out of your raft is back in or on it. If the raft is upside down, you are still in a better position sitting on top of it than you are in the water going down a rapid. It can be hard to get into or onto a raft without assistance, so it's worth practicing in flat water to see what you need to succeed.

Remember that the bow and stern of the raft are higher out of the water then the sides, so go to the side where reentry will be as easy as possible. If your raft is upside down, the ends will actually be lower than the sides, so your best bet is to head to the bow or stern to get on board.

Try to position yourself on the downstream side of the raft so the current isn't pushing your legs underneath the boat. Think of pulling yourself toward the raft rather than straight up. You can give yourself a little boost using the flotation of your PFD if you push yourself underwater and then lunge up and

You can create a kind of stirrup to help people get back into the raft on their own. Here, a piece of webbing has been strung around the stern of the raft to help the guide get back into the boat.

BELLYBAND

A bellyband is a rope or section of webbing that runs along the underside of the raft between attachment points near the oarlocks. The band should be snug to avoid becoming an entanglement hazard and to keep it from snagging on rocks. The idea is simple: The band gives swimmers a strap to pull on to help get on top of the raft in the event of a flip. Some people hate having any extra ropes or lines on their rafts so forgo using a bellyband. If you don't want one, make sure you've practiced getting back on your raft so you know how you'll do it in the event of a swim.

forward, kicking hard. Use the raft handles, D rings, or perimeter line to pull on. Some people hook a flip line onto the raft frame that they can pull on. You can also grab onto drain holes, or use the lacing on a drop-stitch floor for a handhold. If, when you practice, none of these techniques work, you may want to create a small, permanent handle with a loop of webbing that comes out a drain hole on the bottom of the raft to help you up and out of the water. Again, any loop of webbing or rope is a potential entrapment risk, so do this with caution.

If you cannot get on using these tricks, you may need to undo your bow or stern line, and run it through a D ring or around an oarlock so you have something to secure the rope to. You'll then need to head to the opposite side of the raft to try to haul yourself up using the rope. This is not ideal, as you end up with a free rope and swimmers in the water, which is not good. Furthermore, it takes a long time to set the system up. It's best to practice getting on the raft to see if you need to rig some kind of assistance before you end up in a situation where you need to get out of the water.

UPRIGHTING AN OVERTURNED RAFT

Paddle rafts are much easier to upright than a loaded oar rig. They are also easier to flip, so you are more likely to have to perfect your uprighting technique with a paddle raft than an oar rig. But if you are pushing your abilities as a rafter, you are going to flip sometime in your career, so it's important to know what to do.

Once you are on top of a paddle raft, clip the carabiner on your flip line into a D ring on the downstream side of your raft. On an oar rig, attach your flip line to the frame and remove the oars from the oarlocks. If you have a fully loaded raft, you'll probably need a few people on separate flip lines to get enough *umph* to right the boat. Once the flip lines are attached, stand on the upstream tube

HOW TO MAKE A FLIP LINE

Flip lines, or guide belts, can be used for a variety of tasks, including helping you upright an overturned raft. To create a flip line, use a piece of 1-inch tubular webbing that is roughly 10 feet long. (You'll want to personalize the length to fit your torso, so it's best to wait to cut until you know how much you'll need.)

Fold the webbing in half to make a bight. Hold the bight at your navel and wrap the webbing around your waist two times. Tie the two ends together with a water knot and clip the loop into the bight with a carabiner (a locking carabiner is best but not essential). You want the guide belt to be snug to avoid any entanglement issues. You may want to allow a little leeway in the webbing length to account for winter and summer layering. If so, you can get rid of excess length by twisting the water knot a few times to shorten the loop.

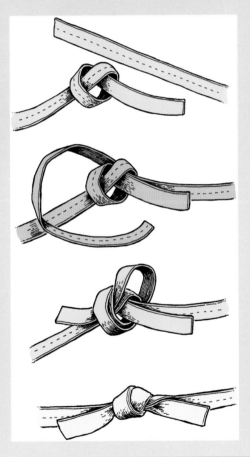

A water knot is used to connect pieces of flat webbing together.

Overturned rafts can be righted from shore. For a lightweight paddle raft, you can attach your rope to two points on the tube farthest from shore and then get your team together to pull until the raft comes over. If your raft is loaded with gear, you may need to attach your rope to two points on the near tube, then run it under the raft and up and over the far tube before pulling. This setup gives you a bit more leverage.
ERIC RILEY, SWIFTWATER SAFETY INSTITUTE

and lean back. One person's body weight is usually enough to upright a paddle raft. It will take more to turn over an oar rig.

Make sure you check over your shoulder for rocks before you try to flip the raft, as you are going to land in the water when the raft comes over.

Some people carry flip lines attached to their rafts. People have different views on this, and there are a variety of systems used. One is to have a flip line stuffed into a bag and hooked onto the oar frame with a carabiner for easy access. Most people go with one bag on each side in this scenario. The trick is to make sure the bag stays closed until you need it open. Again, an extra line in the water is dangerous.

Another technique, commonly used with dories but applicable to rafts, is to have a flip line run from an attachment point on the frame near the oarlock to the bow or stern. In the event of a flip, you can detach the bow or stern point to free the line so you can upright the boat. Again, a flip line on each side allows you to be prepared for whichever way your boat is drifting downstream.

Sometimes this technique is not adequate for a very heavy boat. If you can't upright your raft standing on the tubes, you may have to do it from shore. In this case, attach a rope to the tube closest to shore, run it under the boat and through a D ring or handle on the far side, and then back to shore. Get all hands on deck and pull. This technique allows you to twist the entire raft, and can give you enough leverage to right a fully loaded oar rig.

GETTING STUCK ON A ROCK

Inevitably, you are going to find yourself perched on a rock at some point in your rafting career. Sometimes this can actually be useful. It gives you a chance to pause, catch your breath, and take a look at what's happening around you. Whatever you do, stay calm and breathe. You are fine, just stuck.

Obviously, you don't want to stay on the rock forever. If you have a chance, as the boat hits the rock, try to spin away. This may keep you from getting pinned. If that doesn't work and you are, in fact, pinned, try to figure out exactly where

If your raft gets stuck on a rock in shallow water, you can just get as many people as possible to push it until it's free.

the rock is (or rocks are). This can help you determine the direction you want to try to move the raft. Move people in the raft away from the rock. Try to spin the raft by paddling or rowing on the opposite side. Attach your flip line to the stuck side and attempt to peel the raft off the rock. Get your passengers or crew to help.

If you don't have any luck with these tricks, move to a different part of the raft and try again. Sometimes shifting around can be all that it takes to unweight from the rock and free a raft. If you know one tube is floating freely, you can bounce on it. Beware: If you get a bunch of people bouncing on a tube on top of a rock, you can damage the raft, so only bounce if you know you aren't ramming the tube into a sharp object.

It can help to soften your tubes, so after trying the tricks listed above, release a little air from the raft and see if that helps. If none of these techniques are effective, check to see if it is possible to safely climb out of the raft onto the rock.

If you can climb safely onto the rock that is pinning your raft, you may be able to come up with more options for freeing it. But make sure you have a plan for getting off the rock should the boat come free.

Before you resort to elaborate rope systems to free your raft, try to improvise. Here, rafters are using rope simply to help them gain some leverage in an attempt to free their raft.

From there, you may be able to push the raft off. Plus, getting weight out of the boat may be all it takes to dislodge it. But make sure you have a good plan for getting back in the raft once it comes free. The last thing you want is to leave a bunch of people stranded on a rock in the middle of the river.

If you are still unsuccessful, you may need assistance. Signal to the rest of your party. Sometimes a raft upstream can come down and bump you off a rock. Or you may need to resort to a rope system from shore to get free.

ENTRAPMENT

Most river fatalities involve the use of alcohol, the failure to wear a PFD, and hypothermia—all of which are avoidable errors often associated with people who have no business being on a river. But entrapments are a bit different. They can happen quickly and to people who are armed with the right equipment and knowledge. And they, too, can be deadly.

The defensive swimmer position is intended to help minimize the risk of entrapment, but some data suggests that numbers have actually increased since this position has been emphasized. The reason may be that swimmers are straightening their bodies as soon as they hit the water in an attempt to get onto their backs, putting themselves in vulnerable position with their legs down.

If you take a swim, pull your limbs in close to your body until you come to the water's surface. Then you can assess your situation. You may be able to swim back to the raft. You may be able to swim to an eddy. Or you may need to get on your back and into the defensive position. Don't be passive. Figure out what is happening and actively engage in rescuing yourself.

The danger with foot entrapment is that the current pushes victims forward and holds them there, face down in the water. It can be extremely difficult to dislodge a person against the weight of the entire river. Foot entrapments are a life-and-death emergency.

Your first priority is to establish an airway for your victim. To do this, find a way to prop or pull her face up out of the water so she can get a mouthful of air. If you are in shallow water, you may be able to get a team of people to wade out to the victim and hold her up so she can breathe. You may then be able to give her a PFD or something she can use to support her upper body. These are temporary solutions that literally give you breathing room. But you will probably need to secure a rope across the river and under the victim's armpits to support her more securely while you attempt to get her foot out. Whenever you have a rope across a river, make sure to position someone upstream to alert any boaters coming down of the hazard.

Be creative. You may not need to have the rope attached on the far shore. There may be an eddy that gives you a point midstream for an anchor. There may be a way to attach a rope upstream of the victim. You need to act quickly to establish an airway but then can slow down to figure out the best way to stabilize and eventually free the victim.

Once the victim has a stable airway, it's time to try to figure out how to release her. Unfortunately, there is no guarantee you will be able to do so. The force of the river may be too much. You'll need to be creative to figure out how to release pressure on the foot without undue injury to the victim. That said, there are plenty of stories of boaters breaking someone's femurs to free the person from a pin. In the long run, broken femurs are better than death.

It's all pretty dire. The best thing to do about foot entrapment is to avoid it. Understanding the consequences may help you react appropriately when you find yourself swimming. Keep your feet up and don't try to stand until you are in slow-moving water that is less than knee-deep.

DISLODGING A PINNED RAFT

If your raft is truly pinned, it's not going to come off without some outside assistance. That means ropes. Roped rescues take a long time, so before you start make sure everyone on your team is warm, fed, and comfortable. You will all perform better if those needs are taken care of.

Your next step is to come up with a plan for removing the raft. You have a few options. Here are the two most straightforward ones.

Human-power pull

The simplest rope trick for unsticking a boat is to attach a line to the raft frame and have your entire crew pull on it. This works best if you looked at the situation carefully to assess the best direction of pull to free the boat. Often, a group of ten or more people will be able to dislodge a raft with brute force using this technique. It's simple, easy, and fast.

Vector pull

The next best trick is to try a vector pull. In this situation, one end of the rope is attached to the raft (clip it onto the frame with a piece of webbing and a carabiner) while the other end is clipped into some kind of anchor, such as a tree or boulder. The group then pulls back on the middle of the rope. This creates a simple 2-1 pulley system, giving you a slight mechanical advantage over hauling hand-over-hand. That advantage may be enough to move your boat.

Z-drags

One step up from the vector pull is the Z-drag, or a 3-1 pulley system. The Z-drag is the simplest pulley system, but you can piggyback more pulleys and changes of direction onto it to increase your mechanical advantage if necessary. This book just covers the basics of a Z-drag, but if you plan to boat a lot of technical, Class IV or harder whitewater, you should take a swiftwater rescue course to hone your skills and give you the tools you need to improvise more elaborate rope systems as necessary.

BASIC PIN KIT

- 150-foot, 10 millimeter static rope (approximate diameter and length). You can use your throw rope as long as it is made of Spectra or some material that is strong enough to withstand the forces of a Z-drag. Polypropylene is not sufficient.
- 2 6-foot pieces of 1-inch tubular webbing for anchors onshore and on the raft
- 1 or 2 4- to 6-foot pieces of 6 mm Perlon cord or similar accessory cord to make prusik loops. Make sure the difference in diameter between your prusik cord and the rope is enough for a prusik hitch to bite down and hold under a load.
- 1–2 pulleys
- Minimum of 3 locking carabiners

The first step in setting up a rope system on a pinned raft is attaching the rope to the raft. Make sure you can do that safely before you commit.

Rope Lingo

- Working end: This is the name of the section of rope you are using to tie knots, etc. It's "working."
- Standing end: The standing end of your rope is opposite the working end. As its name indicates, the standing end does not move when you are

working with your rope. The standing and working ends of a rope may flip-flop as you do different tasks. The names are always in reference to what is going on at that moment.

- Bight: A bight is a bend in rope or webbing where the ends do not cross. A bight looks like a U.
- Loop: A loop is a circle in webbing or rope where the ends cross or are tied together. A loop looks like an O.

Building your Z-drag

Step 1: Build an anchor. You will be putting a lot of force on your anchor when you begin hauling your raft, so make sure you find something that is bomber. Trees with trunks larger than 6 inches in diameter or refrigerator-size boulders make good anchors. Make sure to inspect your choice carefully. You're looking to see if a tree is alive and well rooted, or if a boulder is buried in the ground or wedged in place by other rocks. Try to shake or move your anchor choice before committing to it.

Once you find something that will work, tie a loop of webbing around it. Put the webbing low on the anchor. You can use a simple loop tied with a water knot, or you can girth hitch the webbing around your anchor. Check your knots to make sure they are tied properly.

Step 2: Tie a figure eight or overhand on a bight in one end of your rope, and attach it to your raft with a locking carabiner. Consider the angles of your system as you decide where to attach your rope. Ideally you want to avoid having to pull your raft against the main force of the current. Instead, look to use the current to your advantage. With a paddle raft, attach the rope to at least two D rings. With an oar rig, use webbing to tie off to your frame. Again try to get around multiple points.

It can be tricky to get your rope to the raft if it's in the middle of the river. If someone is still on the raft, you can toss a throw bag to the individual. Or, if you have a boat upstream, you might be able to get to the raft that way. Swimming to the raft with your rope is your last resort, and should only be attempted by someone who is experienced swimming in whitewater. At this point, having an experienced kayaker on your team can be really helpful.

Step 3: Place a pulley on your anchor webbing with a locking carabiner. Grab the rope that is coming from the raft and feed a bight through the pulley. Pull the slack out of the rope between the anchor and the raft.

Step 4: Clip a second locking carabiner onto your anchor. Place a prusik hitch on the standing end of the rope (the end going out to the raft) about 10 inches from the pulley. Clip the prusik loop into the second locking biner. This prusik will allow you to reset your Z-drag if you run out of room hauling up your raft. Some pulleys are "self-tending," which means they will block the prusik hitch, preventing it from getting sucked into the pulley. If you do not have a self-tending pulley, you will need to have someone monitor the prusik, keeping it loose until you want to reset the system.

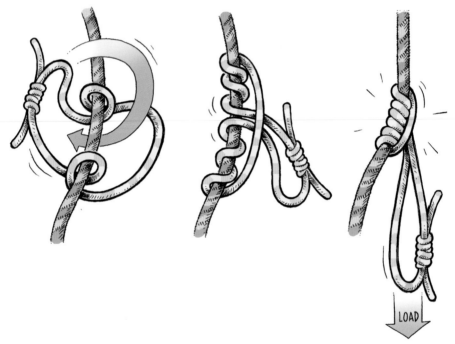

LOAD

The prusik hitch is a friction hitch placed on a rope that cinches down and grips the rope when weighted.

Note: You can use a carabiner rather than a pulley to get the change of direction you need for your Z-drag, but carabiners have more friction and will reduce the mechanical advantage the system gives you.

Step 5: Take the working end of your rope and move down along the standing end as far from your anchor and as close to your raft as possible. Your goal is to get close to the raft to minimize the number of times you have to reset the system. Place a second prusik hitch on the standing end of the rope. Clip a locking carabiner with a pulley into the prusik hitch loop, and feed a bight from the working end of your rope through the pulley. You can use a carabiner rather than a pulley here if that's all you have. Pulleys help minimize the friction in the system so you have more mechanical advantage.

Some rafters like to hang PFDs along the rope between the anchor and the raft. If the rope should break, the PFDs help dampen the shock and keep the rope from snapping back and injuring people.

Step 6: Start pulling. It helps to have a number of people join in to give you more power. Don't wrap the rope around your hands. Remember, it's easy to get entangled in a rope so never, ever, wrap it around yourself. Consider wearing a helmet just in case something breaks and you have stuff flying around.

If you run out of space and still haven't freed your raft, have the prusik minder at the anchor slide the hitch away from the anchor and then have the rest of the team slowly lower the rope until that prusik hitch catches and holds the load. Then slide the other prusik down the standing end of your rope, back

These rafters have set up a simple Z-drag system. Notice the person on the right is minding the anchor prusik so it doesn't get sucked up into the pulley.

Z-DRAG HAZARDS

When you create a Z-drag to move a heavily loaded raft you generate huge forces. If something in the system fails—a D ring pulls, the rope breaks—you suddenly have dangerous projectiles flying around. Remember, gear is always second to human life and limb. If you don't have proper equipment in good condition or the technical expertise to construct a safe Z-drag capable of withstanding the forces you put on it, it's better to leave your raft in place and recover it later with the help of an expert.

toward the raft. Begin pulling on the rope again to make sure the prusik close to the raft catches. This will relieve pressure on the anchor prusik, allowing the minder to release the hitch by working slack into it. He then can slide the hitch away from the anchor so it doesn't get sucked into the pulley or carabiner.

Repeat the process until the raft comes free or you are unable to pull any more rope in.

LAST THOUGHTS ON RESCUE

You can get into trouble quickly on a river, but there are a just few things that you have to do immediately to prevent a disaster—namely, attending to the ABCDEs of first aid. You need to get people breathing in minutes if you want to save their lives, so it's imperative that you act fast. If you're trained in first aid, your actions should be almost instinctual: Survey the scene, get people out of the water, open the airway, check for breathing, check the pulse. If you can't find one of those things, do something about it.

Once you've stabilized your patient, things can and should slow down. Your raft is not going to be any less stuck if you take five minutes to come up with a plan, or with twenty. At NOLS (formerly the National Outdoor Leadership School), where I worked for years, we used to say, "Stop and smoke a cigarette." The saying was attributed to the school's founder, Paul Petzoldt, and the point was not to smoke but to pause, calm down, and weigh your options carefully. After the initial emergency passes you have all the time in the world, so you may as well work methodically to avoid costly mistakes.

As you make your plan, take care to think about whether you can reverse your system. Try not to get yourself into a situation where your only way out is with your knife. Make sure that you are protecting yourself and your teammates. Remember, a rubber raft is not worth anyone's life.

BASIC REPAIR AND MAINTENANCE

Obviously, the best repair is no repair. You can strive for that goal by taking care of your equipment. On river trips that requires a little bit of effort. Sand, wind, sun, and dirt wreak havoc with your gear. One sand granule can plug up a propane stove or a raft valve, as well as make the zippers on your tent unhappy. If you find your gear is starting to perform less than optimally, take a moment to give it some tender-loving care rather than trying to force it.

GENERAL MAINTENANCE

To help prolong the life of your gear, inspect it regularly for damage or wear. Pay close attention to the weak links: zippers, seams, or parts that move around or are exposed to a lot of wear and tear. Wipe down your zippers with a damp cloth to clean the teeth out, especially if you've been camping in dust or sand. If you have Gear Aid, Zip-Tech, or some other zipper lubricant for your dry suit zippers, use some on your tent and other zippers as well to help maintain proper function. Treat the zippers gently when you open and close them.

During your trip, hang your gear up overnight to dry it out, and when you get home take time to clean and dry everything before storing it. Inflate your raft for cleaning. It doesn't have to be super tight, but inflating it speeds up drying in nooks and crannies.

Water-borne invasive species threaten the biodiversity and health of watersheds. You can avoid accidentally spreading these species by rinsing all your boating gear in fresh water (make sure you hose out under your boat tubes and in cracks and crevasses to remove all hitchhikers) and drying it thoroughly for a minimum of forty-eight hours. Make sure you dry your gear out of direct sunlight to avoid UV damage.

BASIC CAMPING REPAIR KIT

- Barge cement or epoxy
- Duct tape
- Seam grip
- Aquaseal
- Fastex buckle to fit various sizes
- P-cord (30 feet)
- Ripstop tape (8 to 12 inches)
- Sewing kit
- Speedy Stitcher
- Tent pole splint with duct tape
- Zipper pulls (5 & 7; 1 each) and zipper stops (1 each)
- Stove replacement parts (pump, valve, cleaning tool, oil, etc.)
- Pliers (vice grip or multitool)

Rinsing and drying will also help preserve your equipment. In some cases you may want to use a mild soap and warm water to get dirt, sweat, sunscreen, insect repellant, and salt off. You can find soap specifically designed to clean and protect high-tech fabrics, including neoprene, at boating and outdoor stores.

Once your gear is dry, store it in a cool, dark place. If you have space to hang stuff up, great. If not, store your paddling gear loosely in a mesh bag or plastic bin. Try not to pack items in too tightly, as over time the material will weaken along folded areas.

But even with the best of care, we all have things happen to our stuff. A spark from the fire burns a hole in your puffy jacket; your raft gets punctured by a sharp rock; or your tent zipper splits. You can take care of these kinds of minor repairs in the field if you have the proper tools and a bit of ingenuity.

CAMPING EQUIPMENT REPAIR

This book does not go into detail on camping equipment repair beyond recommending you pack a repair kit that gives you the tools you need to fix your gear if something goes wrong. It helps to understand how your equipment—such as your stove—works, so when it needs repair you have an idea of what to do.

If you have new gear, make sure you practice with it at home to ensure it's working properly and that you know how to use it. If you have old equipment, check it before you hit the river to make sure it's in good working order. Get in the habit of fixing your gear before you put it away for the season so you don't have lots of work to do before you go on a trip.

RAFT REPAIR KIT

- Small container of solvent such as MEK (methyl ethyl ketone) for PVC or urethane, or Toluol (toluene) for Hypalon
- Tear-Aid tape type A for Hypalon, Tear-Aid patch type B for PVC or urethane. Used for temporary patches.
- Tenacious Tape or Tenacious Tape patches by GEAR AID for dry suit repairs
- Aquaseal for sealing small holes and seams, and for reinforcing stitches. (Aquaseal needs to cure for at least twelve hours.)
- Patches (Hypalon, urethane, or PVC, depending on raft material)
- Glue (type dependent on raft material). Reputable brands include Clifton Hypalon Adhesive, Stabond, and Shore Adhesive. Check with your raft manufacturer if you have any questions.
- Glue roller or roller rasp
- Scissors
- Small-size permanent marker
- Spare air valve(s)
- Valve wrench
- Gloves
- Respirator (especially if working in a confined space)

RAFT AND PADDLING GEAR REPAIR

Materials

As mentioned earlier, raft manufacturers use different materials. It's important to know the type of material you are working with, as this will affect the type of glue you use and how you prepare the material for patching.

Finding the leak

Once you've determined that you have a leak, inspect your raft carefully. Usually the hole will be obvious or in an obvious area, especially if you've hit a rock with your raft. Pinholes that come from general wear and tear are harder to find, but they also won't cause catastrophic deflation, so it's less of an issue in the field. You may just have to pump up your raft more often.

If you suspect you've found the culprit, spray the spot with soapy water to see if you can detect bubbles escaping through the hole. Once you've found your hole, mark the spot with a permanent marker if it is hard to see.

Let the raft dry before you begin working on it.

CLAMSEAL

The ClamSeal is a patented, glueless repair system that repairs small tears or splits in inflatable rafts both above and below the waterline. The system works with two plastic "shells" that screw together to clamp the raft material shut and seal the hole. ClamSeals keep you afloat until you have time to place a permanent patch on the site. The clamps are reusable and are a great addition to any rafter's repair kit. Instructions and diagrams come with the repair kit. There is also an informative video on YouTube (https://www.youtube.com/watch?v=i8dpCcGYNiE).

Temporary repairs

If you are on the water in the middle of a run, you won't have time to go through the lengthy process of making a permanent repair, which generally takes twelve to twenty-four hours for the glues to cure properly.

For quick fixes, Tear-Aid tape or Tear-Aid patches work well. Type A Tear-Aid is for Hypalon rafts, while type B works on PVC or urethane. It's important to use the correct type for your raft to ensure an effective bond.

Start by drying the site thoroughly and cleaning it with an alcohol wipe or solvent. In a pinch, you can use a lint-free cloth. Release air from the tube for repair work. If you apply tape to a fully inflated raft, it will wrinkle when it is deflated, which creates folds that allow air to escape.

Cut a circular piece of tape into a patch that extends roughly 2 inches out from the hole on all sides. Or look for a premade patch big enough to extend 2 inches out. Make sure the patch stays clean, especially along its edges. Apply the patch to the raft and rub it into place, forcing out all air bubbles and warming the patch with friction to help the glue adhere more effectively. If you have a roller in your repair kit, use it to roll the patch down, starting in the center and working your way out to the edges. If you don't have a roller, use a water bottle or something similar to roll out the patch.

For bigger tears, place strips of tape perpendicularly across the tear to hold it together, like you would use Steri-strips to close a wound, before covering the tear with a patch.

Permanent fixes

For more permanent repairs, you will need to allow time for glues to cure. Typically this takes around twelve hours for Aquaseal and twenty-four hours for other glues like Stabond.

KNUCKLE TEST

The knuckle test allows you to determine if your glue is ready. To perform the test, touch the glue with your gloved knuckle. If the glue is ready, your knuckle should stick to the spot, but will come away clean, without leaving a dent in the surface of the glue.

The basic procedure is similar to the procedure you follow for temporary fixes, except instead of tape you will be applying patches made from the material used in your raft. These patches can be purchased from most rafting supply companies. Again, your raft material should dictate your patch material, as the glues have a specific chemical composition that adheres best to the fabric they are designed for.

Clean and prep the site with solvent and then let the raft dry thoroughly. For a pinprick hole, all you need to do is dab a small blob (about ⅛-inch thick) of Aquaseal over the hole. Lay the raft flat so the glue won't run and let it dry for twelve hours.

If you have a tear or a bigger hole, use a patch.

To prep the site, take a piece of 80-grit sandpaper and roughen up a small area around the hole, as well as the underside of the patch. You just want to dull the shine of the material, not grind it down to expose any interior threads. Wipe the spot clean with solvent and let dry.

Different boat manufacturers recommend different glues. Stabond, Vinabond, and Clifton Hypalon Adhesive are examples of reputable brands. Often you can purchase an accelerator for these glues to speed up the curing process and strengthen the cure. Make sure you work outside or use a respirator while using these glues, as they contain known carcinogens.

Coat the surface of the raft and the underside of the patch with a thin layer of glue. Let the glue dry for roughly five minutes, and apply a second layer. (Double-check the directions on your glue container as some glues may need to dry longer between coats.) Let the site dry again—this time wait fifteen minutes, or until the glue is tacky to the touch.

Press the patch on the raft tube carefully, making sure you do not get any wrinkles in the fabric. Rub aggressively with a roller in all directions to warm the glue up so it sticks better. Let the raft sit for twenty-four hours for the glue to cure. You can get back on the water earlier if needed; just know the patch will not be as strong as it will be once the glue has cured, and, therefore, it will be easier to scrape off if you bump up against a rock.

DRY SUIT REPAIR

As with your raft, a hole in your dry suit makes it pretty much useless, so you have to be able to make repairs in the field. You can use a drop of Aquaseal to fix pinprick holes in your dry suit.

For bigger holes in your dry suit, buy a GORE-TEX patch kit with adhesive-back patches. The patches will stick best if you iron them into place. In the field, you can use a Tenacious Tape repair patch or tape to make a temporary fix.

A tear to your gasket is a different story, and needs to be fixed right away to prevent further ripping as you pull the dry suit on and off.

To fix a tear in the gasket, clean the site with an alcohol wipe and let the moisture evaporate off. Cut a piece of Tear-Aid tape twice the length of the rip, plus roughly 1 inch extra. You want the tape to extend beyond the bottom of the tear by half an inch, and to fold over the top of the gasket so it holds the rip on both sides. Trim the edges so the tape is oval-shaped.

Place the gasket on a flat surface with the tear exposed. Peel back half of the Tear-Aid tape backing, and place it ½ inch below the bottom of the tear. Press down on the tape, smoothing it out as you work it toward the edge of the gasket. Once the first half of the tape is secure, remove the rest of the backing. Fold the tape over the edge of the gasket and smooth it down on the backside so the tear is sealed by tape on both sides.

Tear-Aid provides a temporary fix. Keep an eye on it as you pull the gasket on and off. The gasket will stretch more than the tape, so it can come unstuck if you are not careful. If this happens, rub the tape back into place. If the tape has lost its stick, replace the patch.

When you get home, replace the gasket. Tear-Aid won't last long term.

Make sure you apply the glue thinly. Too thick and the patch will be bulky and easy to pull off.

Valve replacement

The principles behind replacing a valve on your raft are similar to what you've already learned about gluing on patches, but you have the added step of removing the old valve and replacing it with a new one.

Tools:
- Replacement valve
- Valve wrench

- Donut patch
- Scissors
- Glue and accelerator
- Mixing container and brush
- Gloves and respirator
- Rag

Deflate the tube until it's soft, and unscrew the broken valve with a valve wrench. Remove the top half of the valve. The bottom half will fall into the tube. To remove it, make two small cuts on either side of the valve hole. This can be scary, as no one wants to cut a raft. Make sure your cuts are just big enough to allow you to get the old valve's backside out. Once you've retrieved the old valve, insert the new backside.

Place the donut patch over the valve hole, and mark where it should go with a waterproof marker. Make a couple of slash marks around the edges of the patch and the tube to help you orient the patch perfectly when you put it in place.

Prep the site and the patch by sanding with 80-grit sandpaper until the shine is gone. Clean both surfaces with solvent (the type depends on material in question) or, in a pinch, with rubbing alcohol. Mix your glue with accelerator.

Check to make sure the backside of the valve is in place properly, and then paint a thin coat of glue over the underside of the patch and the patch site. Make sure you don't get any glue on the inside of the tube. You can place wax paper over the hole to prevent that from happening. Apply three coats of glue, letting it dry for ten to thirty minutes between coats.

Once the final layer of glue passes the knuckle test, place the patch on the tube, checking to make sure the lines you made earlier align properly. Roll out the patch thoroughly in at least four directions to mesh the glue together and remove any air bubbles. Screw the top half of the valve into the bottom half and tighten with the valve wrench. Clean up extra glue with solvent. Wait at least twenty-four hours before inflating the tube. You may need to tighten the valve down further after you inflate the tube.

Scrim shots

You may find places on your raft where the outer coating has worn through and the threads, or scrim, inside have been exposed. This can happen underneath your oar frame or where cargo rubs against the tubes. For small scrim shots, cover the site with a thin layer of Aquaseal. Again, give the Aquaseal at least twelve hours to cure fully. If the site is large, you may be better off applying a patch.

ZIPPERS

More and more rafting gear comes with waterproof zippers. These zippers need to be handled carefully to keep them functioning smoothly. Waterproof zippers are one of the most expensive and time-consuming parts of a dry suit to replace.

Keep the zipper clean. NRS recommends using McNett Zip Care for cleaning. Zip Care comes with an applicator brush, so you just apply it to the zipper and wipe away any excess fluid after you are done. You can also use a toothbrush and warm, soapy water to clean the zipper. The benefit of McNett Zip Care is that it cleans and lubes at the same time, thereby enhancing the movement of the zipper. Brush and clean your zipper after every use if you are paddling in silty or sandy water.

You should also wax the zipper regularly. NRS recommends McNett Zip Tech for keeping waterproof zippers supple and sliding well, but other brands like Gear Aid's Zip Tech work well too. Apply the wax or lube evenly along the zipper, and open and close it a couple of times to work the wax in between the teeth.

The No. 1 cause of zipper failure occurs when the zipper gets bent, causing breaks in the material between the teeth. To prevent this from occurring, store waterproof zippers so they lie flat. If you are transporting anything with a waterproof zipper, try not to bend the zipper too tightly. Pack it loosely and, if possible, without folds or kinks to help maximize its lifespan.

FINAL CONSIDERATIONS

The big thing with repairs is to make sure you've thought through your entire plan before you cut anything. Just like the carpenter's motto: "Measure twice, cut once," double-check before you commit. It's hard to reverse course without needing new materials if you make a mistake. Also, wait to mix up your glue until you are ready to work, as it can become sticky and difficult to spread if you let it sit around too long.

You can remove glue with solvent, which is helpful for cleaning your work site as well as if you misalign a patch. If you think your patch is crooked or has a wrinkle, don't press it down all the way. Apply solvent to a brush and work it into the glue beneath the patch, pulling back gently as you work until the patch is free. You'll then have to start the process over.

For major repairs, you will likely have to send your raft back to the manufacturer. NRS has many helpful videos on basic raft repair on its website, and most manufacturers can answer questions over the phone if you aren't sure what to do with your damaged equipment.

CHAPTER FIFTEEN
DREAM TRIPS

Everyone has heard of the Grand Canyon, and if you are a river rat, running the Colorado through the canyon is undoubtedly high on your bucket list. The Grand is one of the most incredible river trips in the world. Its scenery is spectacular and unique. Its side canyons provide excellent hiking and adventure. Its rapids are exciting and huge, but not as dangerous or technical as some rapids on other challenging whitewater rivers. Plus, the trip is long. You can spend three weeks in the depths of the canyon, far from the maddening crowd and totally cut off from technology, making it the ultimate escape.

Mark Haggerty having the time of his life on his first Grand Canyon adventure.
TOM ZELL

But there are lots of other amazing rivers out there, each with its own unique character and charm; each with its personal advocates who claim it is like no other. The following list of dream rivers is by no means exhaustive or authoritative. I'm sure you will find people who question the merits of the rivers included and excluded, but most people will have at least some of these rivers on their list.

Think of this as a starting point. You can always add your own must-dos to your bucket list as you begin to explore. And this list is in no particular order. All the rivers listed are awesome if you have the skill and experience required to navigate them. Lots of other rivers are awesome, too. Let this list whet your appetite as you start planning your own river adventure.

COLORADO RIVER, GRAND CANYON, ARIZONA

The classic trip through the Grand Canyon starts in Lee's Ferry and ends 226 miles downstream at the Diamond Creek takeout. In between you float through

A three-week adventure through the Grand Canyon is considered by many to be the ultimate American river trip.

Hiking up Havasu Canyon is one of the Grand Canyon's most famous side trips, but there are hundreds of other worthy hikes along the river.
MOLLY ABSOLON

eighty rapids and past ever-changing layers of rock that rise vertiginously from the river's edge and date back hundreds of millions of years. The canyon is known for its side hikes, which include scrambling up the Elves Chasm and wandering past the aquamarine pools in Havasu Creek. The Colorado's rapids are big, rollicking, and fun, and although challenging to run, they end in pools that enable rafters to regroup and rally if they run into trouble. Securing a permit on the Colorado is through a lottery system. Sign up for an account at https://grcariverpermits.nps.gov/login.cfm. Lottery applications are open from February 1-24 for the following year.

MIDDLE FORK AND MAIN SALMON RIVER, IDAHO

The Middle Fork and Main Salmon are two classic wilderness rivers that flow through Idaho's Frank Church–River of No Return Wilderness, the second largest wilderness area in the Lower 48. The Middle Fork is a Class III-IV, 75- to 100-mile run (depending on put-in and takeout), with close to one hundred

The Middle Fork of the Salmon River is a classic wilderness run.

The Middle Fork is known for its clear water, challenging rapids, hot springs, and great fishing.

rapids along its course, while the Main is mostly Class III and flows 84 miles from put-in to takeout, with lots of rapids in between.

A combo Middle-Main trip—known as "turning the corner"—is the ultimate wilderness experience, although it's tricky to secure a permit that allows that adventure.

Both rivers flow through deep-forested canyons featuring wide sandy beaches, hot springs, world-class trout fishing, hiking, wildlife, and spectacular scenery. The Salmon is a free-flowing river, with flows peaking in early summer and dropping off as the season progresses. Both rivers require a permit for their high season, which is obtained through a lottery. For the Middle Fork that season runs from May 28 through September 3. For the Main it's June 20 through September 7. Outside the controlled season a permit is required but there is

Slightly easier than the Middle Fork, the Main is a pool-drop river with big sandy beaches that make excellent campsites.

no limit on numbers. You can obtain a low-season permit through the Forest Service. The Main and Middle Fork lottery opens Dec. 1 and closes Jan. 30 for the following season. Go to the Four Rivers Lottery site at https://www.fs.usda .gov/detail/scnf/passes–permits/recreation/?cid=fsbdev3_029568 for details.

GREEN RIVER, GATES OF LODORE, COLORADO AND UTAH

Starting in Colorado and running down to the Split Mountain boat ramp near Vernal, Utah, this stretch of the Green River is 44 miles long and rated Class III, with one Class IV rapid depending on water levels. The trip is usually done in three or four nights, and flows through the deep red chasm of Lodore Canyon into Echo Park, where Steamboat Rock towers over the river, then into Whirlpool Canyon, and ends in Split Mountain Canyon. The geology along this stretch of river is spectacular, with rock layers shooting up from the river and twisting back down again in torturous folds. Bighorn sheep are common, as are beavers, skunks, black bears, and deer. The camping is on broad sandy beaches

The Gates of Lodore run takes you down the Green River through three separate canyons, starting here at the actual gates.
ERIC SCRANTON

The spectacular geology on display in Split Mountain Canyon on the Green River.
ERIC SCRANTON

sheltered by box elders and cottonwoods. Permits are required during the high season, which runs from May 8 through Sept. 8. Register for the annual lottery between Dec. 1 and Jan. 30 at recreation.gov.

YAMPA RIVER, COLORADO

The Yampa joins the Green in Echo Park, making it possible for the last part of this river trip to overlap with the Lodore trip mentioned above, unless you opt to take out in Echo Park. The Yampa is one of the few free-flowing tributaries to the Colorado River system. It flows through buff-colored sandstone cliffs streaked with "desert varnish" that tower over the river corridor. Camping is on sandy beaches, and side hikes lead up to big vistas that some say rival the Grand Canyon. Known for its archeological sites and wildlife, the Yampa is a four- or five-day trip with Class III-IV rapids. Its season runs from May through July, and permits are secured through recreation.gov's lottery system, which is open from Dec. 1 until Jan. 30.

The Yampa River is one of the few free-flowing tributaries in the Colorado River system.
MOE WITSCHARD

ROGUE RIVER, OREGON

The Rogue River flows through lush Northwestern forests to the Pacific Ocean.

The Rogue River flows out of the Cascade Mountains down to the Pacific Ocean. The classic whitewater run stretches for 35 miles and includes eighty rapids rated up to Class IV in difficulty. The river is surrounded by lush, Northwestern forests renowned for their botanical diversity, huge trees, and abundant wildlife. You are likely to see otters, black bears, deer, bald eagles, great blue herons, and more. Plus, the Rogue is a salmon run, and fishing along its length is world-class. Most rafters take three to four days to run the river. You can stay at lodges along the way, or there are beaches for camping. Permits for the Rogue are obtained through recreation.gov's annual lottery, which takes place Dec. 1 through Jan. 30 for the following season. Permit season runs from May 15 through Oct. 15.

The Rogue trip includes running Mule Canyon, where the river tightens and the rapids start rocking.

SELWAY RIVER, IDAHO

Idaho's Selway River stretches for 47 miles through remote wilderness that is only accessible by boat, foot, or horseback. The river drops 28 feet per mile over the course of its run, creating a highly technical, exciting whitewater adventure with rapids up to Class IV in difficulty. Scenery in the river corridor is rugged and beautiful, and the area is home to elk, deer, black bears, and eagles. The river's crystal clear water hosts a healthy trout population, and the fishing is renowned. Most groups spend two to four nights running the Selway. Permit season for the river runs from May 15 through July 31, when water flows drop, making it impassable for larger boats. Only one trip is permitted to launch per day, adding to the river's wilderness allure. Apply for permits between Dec. 1 and Jan. 31 at rereation.gov.

The Selway River is known for its challenging technical rapids and wilderness character. Only one trip is allowed to launch on the Selway each day during permit season.
COURTESY SOAR NORTHWEST

TATSHENSHINI-ALSEK RIVERS, YUKON TERRITORY, BRITISH COLUMBIA AND ALASKA

The Tatshenshini River offers a consummate wilderness rafting experience. It starts in the Yukon Territory and flows between two towering mountain ranges—the Alsek and Saint Elias—on its way to join the Alsek River and then flow into the sea. You'll float past massive glaciers, through emerald-green rain forests, and by aquamarine icebergs. Wildlife is abundant in the river corridor, and you are likely to see grizzly bears, wolves, moose, and eagles. The run is 140 miles long and is Class II, except for a Class III section through the Tatshenshini Gorge. Most groups take nine days to two weeks to make the trip. Permits are required. To secure a permit, contact the Yakutat Ranger Station in Wrangell-Saint Elias National Park and Preserve. With a $25 administrative fee, your name is put on a list. Each fall permit winners are selected from the list. You can reach the ranger station at (907) 784-3295, or by writing the Yakutat Ranger Station, Wrangell-Saint Elias National Park and Preserve, PO Box 439, Mile 106.8, Richardson Highway, Copper Center, AK 99573. All groups must fly out of Dry Bay at the conclusion of the trip.

ZAMBEZI RIVER, AFRICA

Starting at the foot of Zambia's Victoria Falls, the Zambezi River plunges through 120 miles of Class V rapids at the bottom of a 600- to 800-foot basalt gorge. You have to do a guided trip to run the Zambezi, but it's a four-day, once-in-a-lifetime trip that you'll never forget. This river is big, scary, and fun; add in crocodiles and hippos, and you have quite the adventure in store. In the hands of a trained and talented guide, the Zambezi will have you screaming and laughing as you dive into enormous waves and plow through curling hydraulics. The Zambezi appears on this list because it's one rafters talk about, but it's not for the faint of heart, nor can you run it on your own.

FUTALEUFÚ RIVER, CHILE

The Futaleufú, which is a Mapuche Indian word meaning grand, grand waters, is another big volume, Class V river that draws whitewater boaters from all over the world to northern Patagonia, Chile. The river is known for its turquoise-colored water, spectacular scenery, and raging, nonstop whitewater. Typically run as a series of day trips, the Futaleufú flows through glaciated mountains that rise more than 5,000 feet above the river bottom. The river itself is fast, fun, challenging, and remote. Rafters need to be confident in Class V water to tackle the Futaleufú, but for those who have the skill it's a unique adventure that tops most people's bucket lists.

OTHER THOUGHTS

The world is full of incredible rivers, many of which allow for amazing, multiday float trips. Other rivers that come to mind include the Firth, the Nahanni, or the Chilko in Canada. You can raft the Salt River in Arizona, or the Green through Desolation/Gray Canyons. The San Juan River flows through southern Utah's Colorado Plateau, past ancient Puebloan ruins and through deeply incised canyons. Besides the Grand Canyon, the Colorado offers beautiful, multiday, challenging whitewater trips in Westwater and Cataract Canyons, or you can float through Oregon's remote desert canyons on the Owyhee, Bruneau, or Jarbidge Rivers, all of which are designated Wild and Scenic Rivers. The Illinois River in Oregon is hard, beautiful, and fun, while the Deschutes River is easier and more family-friendly. Each river has its own variables—difficulty, length, ease of access, expense, permits, and season, which affect when and if it is runnable, and each is unique in its scenery and character. You may find your favorite

The Green River through Desolation and Gray Canyons is a great first river trip for new rafters. The rapids start easy and get gradually harder with the toughest being a Class III+.

The Owyhee River cuts a deep canyon through the eastern Oregon desert.

The San Juan River is perfect for families. No rapid is harder than Class II, and there are lots of archeological sites to explore.

river turns out to be one of the more obscure runs just because it is obscure and, therefore, uncrowded.

If you are excited about heading out on your own multiday river trip, it's time to get online and start doing some research. Figure out how to get permits, check in to outfitters, find out the season, look at the ratings, and you are sure to find a trip that meets your skill level, experience, and schedule. And have fun. River trips are the ultimate escape from everyday life. They allow you to relax, recharge, and enjoy being surrounded by nature's splendor.

APPENDIX: FIRST AID AND DRUG KIT CHECKLIST

This checklist comes from the National Park Service's recommendation for a full-size expedition first aid kit for Grand Canyon river runners. Quantities and content should be adapted to the size and length of your trip. (For example, a blood pressure cuff is probably not necessary for most river runners.)

Instruments	Description	Uses
Face mask, pocket mask, or CPR micro shield		Protection for rescuer
Nitrile examination gloves	2–3 pairs	Protection for rescuer
Antimicrobial hand wipes and infectious control bag		Quick clean in absence of soap and water and place to dispose soiled bandages, etc.
Soap (Phisoderm, Hibiclens)	8 to 12 ounces	Antiseptic for wounds
Moleskin	1 package	For blisters
Betadine	1 bottle	For cleaning wounds
Band-Aids	36 (1 inch)	For lacerations
Anti-bacterial ointment	2 tubes	For lacerations and wounds
Butterfly Band-Aids (or know how to make)	18 (various sizes)	For closing lacerations
Carlisle trauma dressing or substitute (feminine napkin, etc.)	3 (4 inch)	For large bleeding wounds
Elastic bandage	2 (3 inch)	For sprains and securing rigid splints
Steri-pad gauze pads	18 (4 inch by 4 inch)	For large wounds
Steri-pad gauze pads	18 (2 inch by 2 inch)	For small wounds

Instruments	Description	Uses
Tape, waterproof adhesive	2 (2-inch rolls)	For sprains, securing dressings, etc.
Triangular bandage or muslin pieces	4 (40 inch)	For securing rigid splints, slinging, and securing extremities, and protecting dressings from contamination
Roller gauze	5 rolls (2 inch by 5 yards)	For holding gauze pads in place, securing splints, and improvising slings
Rigid splint, arm board, SAM splint	1	For inline fracture, pressure bandage
Rigid splint, leg board, SAM splint	1	For inline fracture, pressure bandage
Thermometers (a hypothermia thermometer is recommended)	1 oral, 1 rectal	Diagnosing fever or other exposure illnesses: heatstroke, hypothermia
Stethoscope	1	Diagnostic tool for EMTs and medical personnel
Blood pressure cuff	1	Diagnostic tool for EMTs and medical personnel
Scissors (EMT type)	1 (medium size)	Cutting tape, dressings, clothes
Razor blade, single	2	For removing hair before taping
Tweezers	1	To remove wood splinters, etc.
Safety pins	10 (various sizes)	Mending and triangular bandages.
Cotton swabs	1 package	Cleaning lacerations, eyes, etc.
Pencil/notepad	1 each	Documenting injuries and items used in treatments

Relief of Discomfort

Instruments	Description	Uses
Pain reliever (aspirin or acetaminophen)	36 tablets	Headaches, minor pain, and fever. No aspirin for kids under age 18.
Ibuprofen	200 milligram tablets	Muscle strains, minor pain, or cramps
Antacid	18 tablets	Upset stomach

Instruments	Description	Uses
Antihistamine	18 tablets	Insect bites, colds, hive or rashes. Consider the newer-generation, nonsedating antihistamines like Claritin and Zyrtec, which are dosed once daily and don't make people sleepy like Benadryl.
"Gookinaid" or similar electrolyte replacement drink	1 tub minimum	Relieve or prevent muscle cramps and symptoms of heat exhaustion.
Oil of clove or benzocaine (orabase-B)	1 small bottle	Relief of toothache
Calamine lotion and cortisone cream	1 bottle	Relief of itching from poison ivy, rash, or allergy
Solarcaine	1 bottle	Relief of sunburn pain
Zinc oxide / PABA or sunblock	1 bottle	Prevent sunburn.
Benadryl syrup	1 bottle	Minor allergic reactions
Mild laxative like MiraLAX	Small bottle	Constipation
Kaopectate	Small bottle	Diarrhea
Ophthalmic wash or eye drops	Small bottle	Eye wash / irritation
Ear drops	Small bottle	Clogged / infected ears
Water purification tablets	Small bottle	Purify water on side canyon hikes.
Eye pad	2	Injured eye
Tincture of benzoin	2 small bottles	To hold tape in place and protect skin
Insect repellent	Large can or bottle	Flies, ants, mosquitoes
Monistat	1 tube	Yeast infections
Antibiotics (consult with physician for prescriptions). Consider Zithromax for respiratory infections, Keflex for soft-tissue infections, Cipro for bacterial diarrhea)		On long trips far from medical care, it may be helpful to carry antibiotics, but you will need a medical order from a physician.
Prescription pain medications (Vicodin, Percocet)		These drugs require a prescription from a physician. Consult with your doctor as to whether he or she recommends you carry pain medication on your expedition.

INDEX

ABOUT THE AUTHOR

Molly Absolon has written ten titles for the Backpacker Magazine Outdoor Skills Series (Falcon). She is also the author of *Basic Illustrated Winter Camping*, *Basic Illustrated Alpine Ski Touring*, and *Packrafting*. Molly spent many years working as an outdoor educator for the National Outdoor Leadership School, and her experience teaching beginners technical skills translates on the page into easy-to-read and follow instructions. She lives in Victor, Idaho, with her husband and daughter.